THE
HEART
OF A
GODLY
MAN

About the Author

DR. . GLENN WAGNER
(Ph.D., and D.Lit., Oxford Graduate School; D.Min., Northwest Graduate School) is a dynamic, innovative leader and pastor with more than 30 years of ministerial leadership demonstrating a heart for God's people and a passion for Kingdom growth. Dr. Wagner currently serves as the Executive Director of the Center for Leadership Development and Deployment at University Park Baptist Church and is a founding board member for Promise Keepers, Inc. Having served as senior pastor to four congregations, he has a passion for the training and development of people, especially pastors, which has made him an influential and well sought-after speaker throughout the country and abroad. He has written and contributed to more than nine books including *Your Pastor's Heart, The Church You've Always Wanted, Escape From Church, Inc., God: An Honest Conversation For The Undecided and Fire In Your Bones.* He and his wife Susan have two grown children and live near Charlotte, North Carolina.

Practical Disciplines
for a Man's Spiritual Life

THE HEART OF A GODLY MAN

E. GLENN WAGNER

MOODY PUBLISHERS
CHICAGO

ISBN: 0-8024-3394-4
ISBN-13: 978-0-8024-3394-7

We hope you enjoy this book from Moody Publishers. Our goal is to provide high-quality, thought-provoking books and products that connect truth to your real needs and challenges. For more information on other books and products written and produced from a biblical perspective, go to www.moodypublishers. com or write to:

Moody Publishers
820 N. LaSalle Boulevard
Chicago, IL 60610

5 7 9 10 8 6 4

Printed in the United States of America

To my dad,

Elwood W. Wagner

Thanks for showing me the way.

CONTENTS

ACKNOWLEDGMENTS

The older I get, the more I understand and appreciate how my life and ministry is a composite of people I have had the privilege of knowing over the years. Anything that I might have to offer the body of Christ is because of their input into my life. Their names are too many to mention, but for their faithfulness, I am eternally grateful.

There are several who have contributed to this project that I would like to thank. To Jim Bell of Moody Press, thanks for not only believing in me and the topic of this book, but for helping me to shape it early on and for your contribution to the study guide. My friend Robert Wolgemuth, thanks for staying with me through the peaks and valleys of life and ministry. And a special thanks to Bill Butterworth—your ability to make my thoughts and ramblings make sense is a gift.

To my wife Susan, daughter Haven, and son Justin . . . thanks for the privilege and joy of being husband and father. I love you guys.

THE HEART OF A GODLY MAN

As a pastor and minister-at-large for Promise Keepers, I've been privileged to be around thousands of men over the last few years. There is a movement taking place among men today that appears unprecedented in recent recorded history. Thousands of men are gathering in stadiums and other places. Numerous ministries devoted to ministering to men are being raised up all across our great country. As men, we are gathering into small groups in churches, restaurants, homes, and in lunchrooms in our workplaces.

As I have met many of these men, a recurrent theme is being heard. It's not the theme of a negative response or reaction to the so-called feminization of the American male. But rather we are seeing a genuine hunger among men for reality. And it's the reality that comes from a vital relationship with Jesus Christ. It comes from the understanding that "a man's man is a godly man."

So whether it be in a stadium filled to capacity with sixty thousand, or a church auditorium of three hundred, or a small group of men who meet for weekly accountability and Bible study, there are certain observations I have made that ring true for today's man and his search for reality.

It's been fascinating to discover that every guy is a unique creation of God, with his own blend of personality traits, gifts, and talents. But there is a common factor that I have observed among these Christian brothers. For some it's a fiery passion that burns deeply inside of them, yearning to get out. For others it's the opposite, a more private, personal issue. But we all share the same desire nonetheless. What is this bond we all share in common?

We all want to be *godly men* . . . to go beyond playing the role and to move out of spiritual mediocrity.

Some guys call it "spiritual growth," others refer to it as "maturity," still others name it "Christlikeness." It goes by many different names, but the hope deep inside our hearts rings in unison. We all share the desire, but from there it can get confusing for some of us. Exactly how do I experience this godliness?

The confusion is real, and I want you to know from the outset that I am a guy who can relate to that sort of befuddlement. To give you a specific example, the Bible clearly states to us that confession is good for the soul. So, much as I dread admitting it, I must publicly disclose one of my personal shortcomings that is rather embarrassing . . .

. . . *I hate jigsaw puzzles!*

In contrast, my wife Susan and daughter Haven will spend hours bent over a table in the dining room, looking for that one little piece that will unlock the door to the other four thousand ninety-nine pieces. I admit, I have never been able to "see" what they see and find the appropriate pieces. While I have tried my best to participate, knowing that we would be building a precious memory of quality family time, it didn't take me long to become completely exasperated.

I'd politely excuse myself and go outside to shoot some hoops with my son Justin, who shares my dislike for puzzles, or retire to another room to participate in an activity that I enjoy . . . like reading a good book. At least with a good book, a person can go from a lack of clarity and understanding to a complete picture that is unfolded one frame at a time. Sometimes the book includes suspense and intrigue, but that just adds to the expectation and anticipation.

When it comes to spiritual growth and maturity, I have often felt a similar feeling. I have felt the same frustration, like I'm at a large table pouring over a giant jigsaw puzzle. Others seem to be so excited about the discoveries they're making by finding the correct pieces, while I am still struggling to find the elusive corner piece that will give me hope.

Or maybe it's feeling like Dr. Watson, the well-known sidekick of Sherlock Holmes. The great detective always seems to be able to put all the pieces of the murder puzzle together while we are the last ones to figure it out, even though we have been with Sherlock every step of the way. In fact, it's getting sickening to read "Elementary, my dear Watson!"

It's my belief that the Christian life was never meant to be as frustrating as a jigsaw puzzle or so complex that I am destined to live my life in the shadow of the great spiritual mystery solvers. There's no denying it: there will always be those things that I do not fully comprehend (after all, we are called to walk by faith). But I believe that God has intended that the youngest Christian be able to grow and mature spiritually. In fact, I would go so far as to say that it's even possible for a young child to be mature in the things of Christ.

For, you see, God has provided the means for spiritual growth. It's not an unsolvable mystery or a massive puzzle. We have everything we need to experience the wonder and joy of a growing, dynamic relationship with Jesus Christ. You can look back to see how far you have grown in the things of the Lord. We can solve the mystery and complete the puzzle, because, unlike some of the puzzles at our dining room table, we have *all the pieces* necessary!

THE HEART OF A GODLY MAN:
WHAT IT ISN'T

Before we go too far in discussing what it really means to

know Christ, it might be wise to point out some of the common-
ly held misconceptions. Growing up in church back in the
Northeast, I was able to observe dozens of well-intentioned men
of God who unintentionally led me down a path of confusion
concerning this issue. Back when I was about twelve years old, if
you had asked me what a godly man looks like, I could have described him for you in microscopic detail, based on my observations. He was, quite simply, a *Super Saint:*

—First off, it had to be a guy who brought a Bible to
church.

—The Bible had to be as thick as the Atlanta phone book.

—Once the Bible was opened, every page was well-worn
and underlined with a variety of colored pens and/or pencils.

—Even without his Bible open, this Super Saint could
quote Scripture from memory. And not just a verse here or there;
this guy could recite whole chapters with his eyes closed!

—He was a biblical database. He would talk about Luther
and Calvin like he just had lunch with them the other day.

—He would pray aloud in church. Each prayer would be
filled with "thee's" and "thou's" and "whithersoever thou goest's,"
to the point that most of us had no idea what our brother was
saying!

—His clothing left something to be desired. Whatever was
in style at the time was what this guy *wasn't* wearing. After all,
we're supposed to be "separate from the world," which looked to
me like godliness went hand in hand with the thrift store.

THE HEART OF A GODLY MAN: KNOWING CHRIST

Maybe you are not feeling fulfilled in your life currently:
There isn't an experiencing of the "abundant life" that Jesus described in the Gospels. This may not be happening for you in
some areas of your life, yet you see it in others. Perhaps you feel
guilty because you are not the Super Saint that was described
above. You are stressing because you feel you don't pray enough
or read your Bible like you think you should. You want to do
these things, but you haven't quite figured out how to get it to-

gether. Quite honestly, sometimes it appears completely over-whelming. How can a man move his heart toward God, anyway?

In describing what it means to have the heart of a godly man, the best place to begin is with the Scriptures. The apostle Paul has one of the best summary statements on this issue in all the Bible. Tucked away in prison, Paul wrote these words to the church in Philippi:

> *That I may know Him and the power of His resurrection and the fellowship of His sufferings, being conformed to His death.*
> —Philippians 3:10 (NASB)

The key words to that key verse are the words "know Him." What does it mean to know Christ? One thing is certain—the word that Paul uses for "knowledge" means a great deal more than accumulating statistical and factual information. It's not merely technical knowledge and the gathering of information that draw us into an intimate relationship.

Think of someone close in your life. For me, there is no human more intimate with me than my wife Susan. When we first met back in college, we began to date. There was a bit of learning about one another in terms of where we had grown up, the number of brothers and sisters, what kinds of food we liked, the types of music we enjoyed, and things like that. The "facts" are helpful in beginning to frame a relationship.

But as time progressed and we continued to date, I began to see Susan in a different light. I wanted to get to know her even better, and that was not an intellectual pursuit. It wasn't just the technical and factual knowledge about her that moved me to grow in love with her. It was being in her presence, experiencing her, getting to know how she thinks, feels, and reacts to life that drew me to her. It was the process of moving from the truth about her to a place of action!

It is this sort of experiential knowledge, the intimacy of heart and life, that draws us closer to God, as well. But, like getting to know your date or your mate, knowing Christ follows a pattern that moves us from the more superficial levels of friendship into a relationship of intimacy. The progression follows.

THE HEART OF A GODLY MAN: LEVELS OF FRIENDSHIP

Knowing Christ follows the same path that two people would travel if they were to become good friends. I find it's very helpful to put our spiritual life into the kinds of terms with which we can identify. If following the levels of friendship can assist you in knowing Christ better, then my goal has been accomplished.

There are four levels of friendship that most of us experience as we make contact with people. They also parallel a growing friendship and intimacy with God.

Level One: Initial Friendship

The first level of friendship is the level of an acquaintance. Most of us have many of these sorts of relationships in our lives. When I was back in college, I used to get such a kick out of my buddies who would return from hanging around the center of the campus, watching people walk by. They would occasionally declare, "I just met the most wonderful girl and I *know she is the one for me!*"

If you are looking for a marriage partner, this is not the level of friendship to base your choice on. I'd watch these same guys get their hearts broken because the girls, they discovered, did not have the same feelings in return. Usually the girls didn't see things the same way and this would lead to tension. These guys would end up unloading their dump truck of pain on these poor unsuspecting girls!

Level One Friendship is not the appropriate place to share deep, intimate thoughts and feelings. There's just not enough of a basis to hold those sorts of discussions. At this level we have yet to earn the right to share deeply with them. Sociologists tell us that the average person will greet thousands of people during a lifetime. It is important to be warm and friendly to people, because this is how we will move up the ladder toward more intimate relationships. We begin to gather information and input, looking for common ground in order to pursue a growing relationship.

Level Two: Social Friendship

Perhaps the best way to describe this level of friendship is through a verse in Acts, describing the early church:

> *Every day they continued to meet together in the temple courts. They broke bread in their homes and ate together with glad and sincere hearts.*
>
> —Acts 2:46 (NIV)

Often we reach a certain level in our friendships where we find that we enjoy eating together. (I know I've just struck a chord with men all over the world with that concept!) These are social friendships.

Many people are lonely because they have never experienced this type of relationship. I believe we need social friendships in our lives. When was the last time you met with someone else in this sort of social context? Is this an area that could stand to be improved in your life?

It is important to learn how to be friends and how to nurture friendships. Having friendships with other Christian believers will add knowledge and input to your life. It is vital to your growth in the Lord. We all need social friendships. Go out with people and fellowship with them. You can do it with many people, as evidenced by the testimony of the early church. They constantly took meals together with gladness and sincerity of heart.

Levels One and Two are good, but they don't go far enough. They don't really have the potential to change a life. There is still the absence of trust, which is such a key ingredient. That is why the next level of friendship is so important, yet it is a difficult barrier to cross in many people's lives.

Level Three: Close Friendship

After studying biblical accounts of friendships, I have come to the conclusion that it is usually a great need or a crisis that brings people together at the level of close friendship. While helping a person who is in serious need, you often find that the particular incident brought you closer together even though you might not have been close socially.

When you share in a special need in another person's life, God brings the two of you together and there is something special in your friendship from then on. The book of Proverbs speaks to this:

> *Do not forsake your friend and the friend of your father, and do not go to your brother's house when disaster strikes you—better a neighbor nearby than a brother far away.*
> —Proverbs 27:10 (NIV)

Christians experience this truth. We often discover that our brothers and sisters in Christ are often closer to us than even our blood relatives. It's a great family if all know the Lord, but for many that is not the case. For those, they often find their Christian brothers and sisters more reliable, giving them the friendship they need a lot more than blood relatives.

Think of the classic biblical example of David and Jonathan. Even after Jonathan's death, David took care of one of Jonathan's relatives in his home. David's friendship with Jonathan was so great because God had drawn them together in a crisis and they met each other's needs. That's a close friendship. We can have this sort of relationship, but only with a few people. This is not because we don't desire to have it with many, but because there is a danger in having too many people with whom you share your needs in a time of crisis.

Can a person have close friends besides his marital partner? Absolutely. Scripture encourages it. But there is another level. This should be the relationship between a husband and wife, and it can also be man-to-man or among a group of men in your life.

Level Four: Intimate Friendship

What exactly is an intimate friendship? It involves total acceptance, a dependency on each other, full understanding without judgmental feelings, the absence of pressure on the other person, a sense of protection, and, of course, unconditional love.

Intimate friendship means that your character is in good hands when the two of you are apart. Intimate friends love you at all times, defending you even though they know your faults and weaknesses. They do not expect you to be something you are not. They do not put unnecessary demands and pressures upon you. They are there when you need them; they are there to share in your life. There's nothing you can say to them that they wouldn't understand. They accept and love you, no matter what, regardless of how negative or positive it may be. They are a resource to help you become all that God intends.

This sort of friendship is most often seen through a marital partner. Yet we all need a friend on this level whether we are married or single. That intimacy, that vulnerability, and that transparency are all so vital to our growing spiritual and emotional health.

A close relationship with God follows this same progression. Where are you in the levels of friendship in your relationship with God? Follow the progression of these questions:

Is God an initial friend to me, or is He more?
Is God a social friend to me, or is He more?
Is God a close friend to me, or is He more?
Is God an intimate friend to me?

Please understand there is nothing wrong with any of these levels of friendship. But when it comes to our relationship with Christ, we should be moving toward greater intimacy and not be satisfied with the early levels. It's all about understanding the phrase "to know Him."

As we look at the progression toward greater intimacy in our relationships, the obvious question is, what is necessary to move toward a more intimate relationship? This is what will help us not only in our human relations but also in moving toward our goal of "knowing Christ" in our spiritual journey. These essentials are what the spiritual disciplines are designed to bring to us.

THE HEART OF A GODLY MAN:
ESSENTIALS FOR INTIMACY

There are many qualities one should possess for an intimate relationship, and the same qualities speak of how the Lord acts toward us. The list is long, but let's name just a few of them.

• Confidence

It is important to begin with this characteristic. I don't know how many times I have heard from people that they have dealt with personal hurt and disappointment because one of their intimate friends shared something they had wanted kept in confidence. Before too long, that intimate friendship begins to deteriorate. Proverbs states:

> He who covers over an offense promotes love, but whoever repeats the matter separates close friends.
>
> —Proverbs 17:9 (NIV)

He who covers a transgression is seeking love, but he who repeats the matter is going to separate intimate friends. Confidence is the vital factor in this relationship. In order to build a friendship at this level, there must be protection and the defending of the relationship. Do not share with others what has been shared with you in private. It builds trust.

• Confrontation and Care

Balance is the key issue here. Confrontation must be linked with care for the individual, as well as commitment to a positive outcome. This is a difficult dimension of intimacy, but an important one, nonetheless. "Wait a minute," I can hear someone say. "I don't want a relationship that includes arguing and fighting!" I agree, but confrontation is something different. Again, the book of Proverbs is helpful:

> Better is open rebuke than hidden love. Wounds from a friend

can be trusted, but an enemy multiplies kisses.

—Proverbs 27:5, 6

The New Testament also speaks about this issue:

But speaking the truth in love, we are to grow up in all aspects into Him who is the head, even Christ.

—Ephesians 4:13 (NASB)

Some people don't believe in confrontation because they don't want the hassle. They don't want to bring anything into the relationship that will be perceived as a threat. But, the failure to confront is an indication that there's a lack of love. They're not loving the other person in the way God wants them to love the other, but they are rather protecting themselves.

In a former pastorate, I had a dear older woman who would confront me on a fairly regular basis. She would either march down the aisle after the service or call me later in the week on the phone. If she was going to confront me, she would always start with, "Now, Glenn . . ." Not, "Now, Pastor . . ." but "Now, Glenn . . ." Anytime someone over seventy calls you by your first name, you better listen! But I always knew she was coming to me because she loved me. She was concerned about my ministry and its direction. She always connected confrontation with care.

The key is coming to the issue of confrontation with a heart filled with love and humility. It makes all the difference in the world. Confrontation is not easy, but it is essential. So often we are sincere and enthusiastic, but we lack the ability to restore things when they go a bit off course. This is why confrontation is so significant to the health of an intimate relationship.

• *Counsel*

Who do you go to when you need wisdom, insight, and advice on a weighty matter in your life? The first answer on the human level should be the person in your life that you consider your intimate friend.

Perfume and incense bring joy to the heart, and the pleasant-

ness of one's friend springs from his earnest counsel.
                                                —Proverbs 27:9 (NIV)

The counsel you receive from your intimate friend is what gives you the encouraging, the exhorting, and the admonishing that truly stretches you to your full potential. The verse above is like saying counsel is the deodorant we all need! It is sweet when someone gives you that kind of encouragement.

One of the practical suggestions I often make to people who are desiring greater intimacy is to learn how to ask questions of each other. It is in the asking of these questions that we often learn deeper, more profound insights into one another. It can be very rewarding.

• *Companionship*

God established this element at the very beginning of human history. The book of Genesis records:

The Lord God said, "It is not good for the man to be alone. I will make a helper suitable for him."
                                                —Genesis 2:18 (NIV)

Companionship involves a lot more than two people being in the same place at the same time. I once had a man tell me that when he went out to dinner with his wife, he still felt like he was eating alone. There was nothing there. They don't have a friendship, and I hurt for that man.

On the other hand, I had a woman once tell me, "I enjoy being with my husband so much! He is so exciting to me. Other people think he's a dud, but not me. They see him as quiet and boring, but they just don't know him like I do!" That couple has something special. If the two of you are having a great time, what difference does it make what other people think?

Companionship is vital. Spiritually speaking, it is a comfort to know that the Lord is always with us. I recall hearing a soldier recount his Vietnam story of being imprisoned in a POW camp. The worst punishment of all was not any sort of physical torture—it was being separated from everyone. In those long, lonely hours of painful, solitary confinement, this dear Christian man tapped into his most intimate Friend, God Himself.

Isn't it great to know that when things are going on in your life that no one else knows about, you have Someone there to help you who knows you and loves you? Just being together is all that is needed to heal the hurt and meet the need.

• Consistency

Where are you when your friend really needs you? The most intimate of friends is there for his friend.

> *A friend loves at all times, and a brother is born for adversity.*
> —Proverbs 17:17 (NIV)

This is a verse all about consistency. It's knowing that part of an intimate friendship is being there for the other person, not just when it's convenient, but in the inconvenient times as well.

This quality often diminishes over the years in our human relationships, if we don't keep an eye on it. That's one other issue we never have to worry about in our intimate relationship with the Lord. He is always there, no matter what. It's the beauty of His consistency.

• Commitment

> *A man of many companions may come to ruin, but there is a friend who sticks closer than a brother.*
> —Proverbs 18:24 (NIV)

This verse teaches us that too many friends will often bring harm to an individual. It is impossible to be close to many people at once. It has a tendency to break you down emotionally. But the last part of the verse tells us about the value of a single friend. Actually, the Hebrew word used there is the word for "lover." There is a wonderful lover who sticks closer than a brother. He or she clings to you even more than a blood brother would.

I believe the primary teaching of this verse is for another

human being, a fellow human friend. But of course, it also has a spiritual application in referring to the Lord in our lives. He is the dearest Friend we could ever have. And He will be committed to us always.

Commitment is such an out-of-date concept in our world of permissive, irresponsible escapism. There are many who would rather run than stick with it, rationalizing themselves in and out of relationships. But commitment is a key element in intimacy.

So, how do you measure up against this list of essentials? Are you moving toward intimacy with God because of these elements in your life? Think about these questions:

Do I have confidence in the Lord?

Does God have confidence in me?

Am I willing to allow God to confront me concerning problem areas in my life?

Do I listen to the Lord's counsel?

Does God listen to me?

Is God Someone I would consider my companion?

Does God consider me His companion?

How am I demonstrating the kind of consistency that He displays to me?

Am I truly committed to the Lord?

Is the Lord truly committed to me?

THE HEART OF A GODLY MAN: PREREQUISITES FOR INTIMACY

A legitimate follow-up question to the levels of friendship would be: "What should I do to move from a more shallow relationship to one of more intimacy?" Unfortunately, men are known for their difficulty in making any sort of movement away from superficiality. Nonetheless, there are concrete, practical steps a guy can take to make intimacy a reality.

I am indebted to my good friend Dr. Rod Cooper for

putting together this list of qualities necessary for someone to move from isolation to intimacy. Possessing these six qualities will ensure that we can move into a relationship without a great deal of "baggage."

1. A Solid Self-Image
2. Empathy
3. Loyalty
4. Trust
5. Delay of Gratification
6. Boundaries

It's worth noting that each of these six qualities corresponds to traits found in the character of God. He is secure in Himself, He understands us, He will never fail us, He can be trusted, He is willing to wait for the fulfillment of His will, and He will never push Himself on us.

THE HEART OF A GODLY MAN: WORTH THE EFFORT

My mother's father was an excellent musician. One day when I was young, our family was visiting my grandfather. I remember that the occasion was the recent death of my uncle. After dinner, Grandpop, in need of a very serious talk, sat down with my brother and me.

"Boys," he began, "ever since your uncle's death, I just don't feel like playing my trumpet anymore."

My brother and I looked at one another with helpless and confused expressions. After all, I was only five years old at the time, so I had no idea where he could be going with a conversation of this nature.

"So," he continued in sober tones, "what I want to know is, which of you two boys would be willing to take my place? Who wants to become the new musician in the family?"

"I will, Grandpop!" I volunteered.

With that, his serious face burst into a smile whose warmth

radiated throughout the little room. "Glenn, I have something for you," he said as he carefully pulled from behind the chair a well-worn case.

"What is it?" I asked curiously.

"It's my trumpet."

I swallowed hard, knowing this was an incredible gift. But it was just the beginning of my grandfather's gifts to me. For along with the trumpet, he arranged for me to begin lessons with a wonderful teacher who was an old friend of his. What my grandfather really gave me was the gift of music. He took me to concerts in the park and at the local concert hall. Often after one of the concerts, we would go backstage, where Grandpop would introduce me to some of his musician friends. As I would listen to them converse, invariably one of the musicians would recite Grandpop's favorite maxim concerning music: "If you miss a single day of practice, you will know it. If you miss two days of practice, your teacher will know it. If you miss three days of practice, everybody will know it."

Unfortunately, I would have many times in my trumpet playing career where I would miss more than three days. Oh, I was able to be disciplined for short periods of time, especially if I had a solo number in a concert (I guess I didn't want to embarrass myself!). But I was never able to sustain the discipline necessary to become a really great musician.

I was good, I had potential, but I never became great.

In contrast to that story, my daughter Haven at one point in her life pursued figure skating and ice dancing. She put me to shame in terms of personal discipline. She would spend five or six days a week at the ice rink in order to improve on her skills. And I have never recalled an occasion where we had to remind her to practice. Actually, we had to encourage her to "take a vacation" once in a while! She was very focused, very disciplined, and very committed to making her run at the Olympics someday.

While that dream has been interrupted, she continues to show the ability to discipline herself to reach a goal.

It's the same inner strength the apostle Paul spoke of when he encouraged believers to "discipline ourselves for the purpose of godliness." My guess is, that's why this book is in your hands right now. For this is a book for men who want to strengthen their spiritual hearts and grow in godliness, setting a course toward the ultimate goal of knowing Christ.

Throughout the history of the church, the tools best gathered for the accomplishment of this goal have been referred to as the *spiritual disciplines.* Historians and theologians have compiled them into various lists and sublists. But for our purposes, we are going to look at the following:

- Bible reading
- Bible study
- Bible memorization
- Bible meditation
- prayer
- worship
- fasting
- solitude
- journaling
- giving
- communicating our faith
- accountability

This is not an attempt to reduce godliness down to a slick formula or lifeless prescription that can be taken like candy-coated medicine. Nor is it a list of chores to be checked off as if they were nothing more significant than cutting the grass or taking out the trash. But it is a serious attempt to discover the reality of that which we men are desirous. I honestly believe that through the consistent application of these types of disciplines, we will come to discover what it really means to have the heart of a godly man. Let's begin our journey together.

Trust me, it'll be worth the effort.

CHAPTER ONE

NOT A SPECTATOR SPORT

Why is it that we Christian men are often content to be saved, slip into church on Sunday, slump down, slumber, and slither out at the appointed time (whether the service is over or not)? Why are we so willing to be spectators in the kingdom and consign ourselves to a life of spiritual mediocrity?

Wouldn't it be more exciting to be in the middle of the action, placing ourselves in the center of God's work in this world? Yet most of us remain firmly planted on the sidelines. Why don't we get up and get involved?

Maybe it's because we have either a fear or a misunderstanding (or both) of what it takes to develop the heart of a godly man.

What *does* it take? Discipline.

Isn't it interesting that even the least-talented players on a team still want to get into the game? In high school, we had a guy on our basketball team who, while he was a great friend, just didn't have much ability. But Kevin always wanted to play. He loved the game. On one occasion, he was begging the coach to let him play.

Finally, with only a few minutes left, the coach motioned

for Kevin to go in. Realizing this was his moment, he hurriedly pulled his warm-up jersey over his head. In his excitement, he didn't realize he had pulled off his shirt as well! Believe it or not, Kevin didn't know it and ran onto the court bare-chested.

In the church today, we don't have many Kevins running up and down the sidelines, begging the coach to put them in. Perhaps the reason is this issue of discipline.

Personally, I hate the word *discipline*. It's not a concept that fills me with warm fuzzies. Instead, it's a constant source of stress in my life.

Like most men I know, I do have areas of my life where I'm disciplined. In my work and ministry, for example, I have an entire chain of occupational disciplines linked together with no problem whatsoever. I live in the context of deadlines, agreements, meetings, and delivering what I promised. I can run my daily routine by a schedule and Day-Timer as well as the best of them. Advanced planning fits me like a well-tailored suit of clothes.

Yes, I'm well disciplined on the job. But then there's my *personal life*, which is quite another story. OK, I'm not a complete failure, but I do have two areas that embarrass me: physical exercise and getting projects done around the house.

I know all about the importance of caring for our bodies. My buddies are playing racquetball, working out at the gym, playing basketball during their lunch hours, or jogging nine miles before breakfast. I just can't seem to work up the personal discipline necessary to join in those activities. I tried jogging, but I noticed while running that I've never seen a jogger smiling. Why would I do something that makes people miserable? So I took up golf . . . and I "ride" whenever possible.

Then there's the whole issue of working on projects around the house. Susan is so disciplined about making the Honey-do list; why can't I muster the discipline to complete the tasks? I don't know which is worse, never getting to projects or starting projects but never finishing. Either way, my track record on personal discipline leaves something to be desired.

I'm actually getting better in these areas. I'm slowly but

steadily knocking items off that to-do list, and I'm also doing a pretty good job of exercising in order to keep my weight down. But even when I'm making progress, discipline involves a struggle.

DISCIPLINE: NEGATIVE OR POSITIVE?

Discipline gets a negative rap a good deal of the time. In his book *Personal Religious Disciplines*, John Edward Gardner discusses the damage done by this sort of thinking:

> *If a spiritual discipline is employed primarily as a restricting and restraining factor in human behavior, it will not be helpful. Unfortunately, discipline has often been interpreted in terms of correction and punishment. While these may be very appropriate by-products, they are little more. When the objective of discipline is primarily to purge the self, the most likely development is the creation of a spiritual void. Properly conceived discipline must be positive and creative. In order to produce wholesome benefits, it must provide for him who practices it a sense of gratification, satisfaction, and fascination.*[1]

That was a refreshing paragraph for me to read. Why do we men find the concept of discipline so intimidating, so threatening, so impossible to attain? Certainly Gardner is on target with his comments concerning our thinking of discipline as restraining and restricting. But that just adds to the feeling that being a man of God is out of my reach.

In terms of the disciplines of godliness, I can recall thinking as a teenager how impossible it would be for me to fulfill them. I decided at an early age that I could never become a preacher. *I'm not spiritual enough,* I concluded. The men I saw at the front of the church could preach circles around me, pray me into oblivion, and recite from memory the entire list of foreign missionaries whose pictures were hanging in the narthex.

ORDINARY MEN USED OF GOD

But the Scriptures give us a much different picture. Look more closely at the men of the Bible. They weren't perfect plaster statues on pedestals. They were real, live, flesh-and-blood guys, complete with their shortcomings and imperfections. Yet they were used mightily of God.

Consider a few examples:

- Paul: Before his conversion, he zealously persecuted God's people; afterward, he could experience the joy of the Lord while enduring the pain of imprisonment for his faith.

- Job: His is the classic story of a regular guy who loved God and was put through trials beyond belief. He dared to question God, but he still said, "Though he slay me, yet will I trust in him" (Job 13:15 KJV).

- Nehemiah: He served in the house of a pagan king, yet God used him to lead the entire nation of Israel in rebuilding the walls around Jerusalem.

- Gideon: At one point he was hiding in fear; then God called him to defeat Israel's enemies and restore its freedom.

- David: In weak moments, he could commit adultery and murder. Yet for most of his life he was a man after God's own heart.

- Noah: Nothing seemed out of the ordinary about this man until the earth was flooded and the only way of rescue was the ark he had built in obedience to God's command.

- Peter: Talk about an average guy! Here was a man who constantly struggled with his temper, with speaking without thinking (usually opening his mouth just long enough to take one foot out and put the other in), and with a variety of other common shortcomings. Yet he also became an apostle and the author of two books of the Bible.

On a recent trip to Russia, I met with a group of pastors, discussing men's ministry in the local church. During one of the meals, my interpreter asked if I had met "that pastor." He pointed to a short, slight, bearded man who had just entered the room. I replied that I hadn't. So he went on to tell me the man's story. The bearded man's son now pastors the church the father founded. But before the fall of communism, the man had spent twenty-four years imprisoned in Siberia.

The police had come to him one day to inform him that he must stop preaching. He listened carefully to what they had to say, but then he informed them that he must obey God rather than man. The next Sunday, he was in Siberia. He was released after eight years, again with orders not to preach. His reply was the same as before.

He preached the following Sunday, was immediately arrested, and was sentenced to another eight years in prison.

After his second release, he was once again cautioned against preaching. Again he replied that he must obey God. Again he preached. Again he was sent to Siberia.

This "small" (he was about 5'3") man had great passion and commitment. Today he's more than eighty years old and bent from the ravages of prison and age. But if you look into his eyes, you can see the fire that still burns in his soul. Such passion and commitment take the one the world calls "ordinary" or "insignificant" and make him great in the kingdom of God. Such were the passion and commitment of a prophet like Isaiah or an evangelist like Paul.

We need that same passion and commitment to the Lord in our daily lives.

At a church I once pastored, I brought in a guest speaker for a series of special meetings, and, like most guest speakers I know, he was passionate about his subject. In the midst of an emotional portion of his message (not to mention loud!), he asked the congregation a series of questions:

"Are Christians people of the Book?"

"Are Christians people of prayer?"

"Are Christians people of worship?"

"Are Christians people of fellowship?"

To all those questions, the congregation replied with hearty "Amen's!" But he had an important point to make: "If these things are so, why do so many who say they are Christians live like non-Christians in these areas?"

We often suggest that a person is living like a non-Christian when he's doing certain things or committing particular sins. But this man was showing that, fundamentally, to live as a non-Christian is to neglect disciplines such as Bible reading, prayer, worship, and fellowship—the resources God has provided to enable us to live godly lives.

The church needs Christians who are passionate about and committed to their faith and willing to get involved.

THE PASSION OF INVOLVEMENT

"I'm just not the kind of guy who likes to get involved" is a comment I hear regularly. It usually comes from a man who is trying to be honest. He doesn't see himself as an extroverted, high-energy, make-a-big-splash sort of guy. I appreciate his candor, but a closer look may reveal another side of this quiet brother.

The truth is, all of us are aggressive about many things. Do you relate to any of the following?

- *Politics.* The mere mention of the word can set the shyest person off on a tirade about what's right or what's wrong in his country!
- *Vocation.* Here's a great example of involvement. One of our goals as a man is to discover our vocational calling in life and then pursue it with vigor.
- *Sports.* OK, it's a male cliché, but it really is true. I know guys who sit quietly in most other contexts, but put them in a stadium or in front of a television showing their favorite team in action and they nearly climb the walls with the excitement of being involved in the game, not to mention knowing much more than the coach about what their team should be doing.

- *Music.* Want to know how to divide a room quickly? Ask people to clarify their personal tastes in music. This is especially dangerous in a Christian setting. I've seen churches split over the issue of "contemporary music" versus "traditional music." This topic generates plenty of energy, passion, and conviction. I just wish it wasn't at the price of unity.

- *Spiritual growth.* OK, I tried to sneak this one past you. Granted, this is not something we normally think of when we consider aggressive, active participation, but I hope I can change your point of view.

Sometimes God uses circumstances or even a tragedy to move us into involvement. On several occasions, I've had the privilege of ministering at St. James Church in Cape Town, South Africa. You may have heard of this great church and its pastor, the Rev. Frank Retief. It has had a powerful impact in South Africa and is known as a church that reaches beyond the barriers of race and culture.

On the night of July 25, 1993, during the evening service, the door next to the stage burst open just as a duet was finishing its ministry in song. A man stood in the doorway in dark clothing, with an R4 automatic weapon in his hands. People were stunned. Was this a drama presentation? Was this man merely a late arriver? Unfortunately, the gunman began spraying bullets across the congregation. The injured screamed and cried out for help. Others dove for cover.

Next, the gunman tossed a grenade that had been taped to a can of nails into the congregation. The explosion sent nails and shrapnel everywhere. Fifty-three people were wounded. A young man lost his life as he covered his two friends to protect them. A young mother of three children was also killed.

Whenever I have the honor of being at St. James, I'm overwhelmed with what God has done through that tragedy. For example, Pastor Retief told me the story of one black man who had been sitting near the front when the attack occurred. As people dove for the floor, he was inadvertently pushed into the aisle.

While seeking cover, he felt something hit his back, and he felt his right leg go numb. He said, "That's OK, God. I'll serve You with one leg!" Then he felt something hit his back a second time. This time his left leg went numb. His response? "That's OK, God. I'll serve You with no legs!"

This man sat down in the front pew at the service I was in. He has permanent physical and emotional damage, yet one thing is still true—he is not on the sidelines. He's committed to being a player on the field for the cause of Christ.

What is the common factor arching over all these issues? It's *passion*. It's the feeling inside us that moves us from the couch to the field. We can be that aggressive, that passionate about spiritual growth, too. It's not too much to ask. God can make it happen.

WARNING: POSSIBLE DANGER AHEAD

A young man was walking home late one night and decided to take a shortcut through a cemetery. In the darkness, he stumbled into an open grave. He yelled for help until his voice grew faint with the strain. No matter how loudly he screamed, no one was there to help him.

He tried climbing out of the grave, but it was too deep a hole. His arms and legs grew weak from exhaustion. Completely worn out, he eventually decided to sit in a corner of the grave, waiting until the cemetery workers showed up in the morning.

A short time later, another guy who had wanted to take a shortcut fell into the same open grave. Just like the first guy, he began screaming for help and trying with all his might—yet without success—to climb out of the grave.

Suddenly, the second guy heard a voice from one of the dark corners of the grave tell him, "You can't get out of here!"

But he did!

It's all about motivation.

Unfortunately, it's possible to be motivated to do the right thing and yet use the wrong method. That's apparently what was happening in the churches in the region known as Galatia in New Testament times. The apostle Paul had to write them in order to correct their methodology. They had adopted a method that has come to be known today as Galatianism.

Simply put, Galatianism is the mistaken belief that we can grow in godliness through legalism—that is, through following a set of rules ("the law"). We can take the good things, the tools and resources of the spiritual disciplines, and bind ourselves into a system of works and law-keeping. As Paul instructed the Galatian believers, however, we don't pursue the spiritual disciplines and growth in godliness through our own efforts, but through the empowerment of God's grace.

Are we law keepers or grace keepers? That's a question worth addressing, because in the long run, it's *grace* that produces motivation to godly living. The central passage in Galatians that speaks to this issue is at the end of the second chapter:

> *I have been crucified with Christ; and it is no longer I who live, but Christ lives in me; and the life which I now live in the flesh I live by faith in the Son of God, who loved me and gave Himself up for me. I do not nullify the grace of God, for if righteousness comes through the Law, then Christ died needlessly.* (Galatians 2:20–21 NASB)

This passage teaches us four motivating truths about grace.

1. The position we have in Christ. The concept in verse 20 that "I have been crucified with Christ" is extremely important for us to grasp. In the original Greek in which the New Testament was written, the phrase is in the perfect tense, signifying something that happened in the past and continues to have an effect in the present. When we refer to things in the English past tense, it just means something that happened back in time. But the Greek perfect tense in this phrase points to the fact that we *were* crucified with Christ back at the cross, and we *are still*, right now, crucified with Christ. Nothing has changed.

The phrase "crucified with" is used elsewhere in the New Testament to refer to the thieves who were hung with Jesus. What a beautiful illustration, because positionally, in God's eyes, we were there at the cross of Christ, just like those thieves! We have all been, at one moment in time, crucified with Christ. When He died on the cross, we all died there with Him. His death has already been accomplished for all of us. We need to believe that this is our position before God.

In the book of Romans, Paul said it another way: "For we know that our old self was crucified with him so that the body of sin might be rendered powerless, that we should no longer be slaves to sin—because anyone who has died has been freed from sin" (Romans 6:6–7 NIV).

We are freed from sin. *Freed* means to be justified, declared righteous. Paul was saying that since we're dead, we won't be slaves to sin anymore. We have been delivered from its power. It's powerless in our lives. Do you believe it? It's true, you know. The position we have that we must understand is that we've been crucified with Christ.

2. The presence of Christ in us. Not only have we been crucified with Christ, but we must also realize we are *resurrected* with Him. The Bible teaches in Galatians 2:20 that there's new life within: *"Christ lives in me."*

Sometimes I begin my day with a prayer: "Lord, help me remember today that there's new life in me. It's not the old life dressed up a little bit, but the very life of God is now in me. Make me aware of that truth this day."

Yet this life can be forced to lie dormant if we live in our own strength, not allowing God's power to work in us. And in doing so, we sin against the truth that God asks us to believe—that Christ lives in us.

Do you believe Jesus is alive in you right now? The spiritual disciplines will flow more smoothly from your life if you're living with an awareness of the presence of Christ in your daily life.

3. The pattern of faith. Paul also talked about "the life which I now live." How is it to be lived? By faith, trusting in the Son of God, who loved us and gave Himself for us. We don't live this life now (present tense) by our works, by obeying the Law, by busyness, or by Christian "activities." We live this life by faith in the Son of God.

I like to think of faith's pattern this way: First, it's a response to the incredible gift of love God gave us when He sent Christ to become our Savior. The most significant demonstration of that love was the Cross, where all was accomplished and finished for us.

Second, faith is receiving the truth. We must receive in order to appropriate this pattern in our own lives. We're to live in the glory of the fact that the Son of God gave His life for us, paying the penalty we deserved for our sins.

4. The problem we face. "I do not nullify the grace of God, for if righteousness comes through the law, then Christ died needlessly," Paul taught in Galatians 2:21 (NIV). The phrase "died needlessly" means "died without cause." But Christ's death was *not* without cause, Paul said, because it was for us! If His life and righteousness could be produced by our works, that's when we would have to conclude He died for nothing.

Jesus died to give us His righteousness and to free us from the bondage of the law. The more we believe this, the more real it will become in our lives. It's vitally important, as we embark on a discussion of the spiritual disciplines, to get this truth nailed down. We can't do this stuff the way God wants us to by generating it out of our flesh. It's time to trust in God's power.

It's sad to think of all the guys who are walking around acting, playing the role of the good little Christian. God is saying, "Relax, men. Stop it. Instead of your act, just remember that at the cross, I did it all. Stop trying to prove yourselves!"

Get into the Bible. Read it and meditate on it until you're filled with excitement and joy over all the Lord has accomplished for you. Then trust it; rest in its truth. We have been crucified with Christ. We're not chained to the law, with its accompanying bondage and guilt.

We have been set free in Jesus Christ.

THE IMPORTANCE OF ACCOUNTABILITY

One of the secrets of steady spiritual growth is understanding that God never intended for us to do it all by ourselves. Encouragement can be found through the lives of fellow travelers. Men in our circle of influence, in a relationship of mutual support, can assist us in moving toward our spiritual goals.

This principle of accountability to one another is such a vital element in our success that I devote an entire chapter to it later in the book. For now, however, suffice it to say that a man needs someone, or a group of someones, who will affirm him, encourage him, challenge him, correct him, and help him stay on course.

CHAPTER TWO
WHAT'S IN IT FOR ME?

We've seen that it's passion for God that will fuel our desire to pursue godliness, and that our pursuit is through God's grace. Now let's get practical. It may sound a bit selfish, but it's still valid to ask concerning spiritual disciplines, "What's in it for me? Why *should* I pursue godliness?"

The apostle Paul wrote,

> *But have nothing to do with worldly fables fit only for old women. On the other hand, discipline yourself for the purpose of godliness; for bodily discipline is only of little profit, but godliness is profitable for all things, since it holds promise for the present life and also for the life to come.* (1 Timothy 4:7–8 NASB)

I don't know many people who will give themselves to something until they understand the benefits. After all, isn't that the basic premise of all advertising and sales techniques? Sometime today, your children will be absolutely convinced by some overpaid spokesperson on television that their lives won't be worth living unless they own something like the latest pair of sneakers, which happen to cost $150! They need them to run faster, jump higher, and feel better about themselves. They're convinced that the benefits far outweigh the price. Dad's response? Get over it or get a job! We marvel at how easily our kids are taken in.

But don't be so smug. When they show the ads for tools or cars or the latest razor that will have women swooning, it'll be our turn to respond. Wake up, dads! We're also motivated by "the benefits," whether real or imagined. So I want us to look at the *real* benefits of godliness and spiritual maturity. No false advertising. As Joe Friday would say on the old *Dragnet* show, "Just the facts."

THE BENEFITS OF THE SPIRITUAL DISCIPLINES

As we look at the benefits of being involved in the spiritual disciplines, realize that this list is by no means exhaustive. But it should stimulate our thinking in the right direction.

The abundant life

Jesus said, "I came that they may have life, and have it abundantly" (John 10:10b NASB). This promise to His followers is more than a trite cliché. He never intended for us to struggle along on our own, hoping that one day we'd make it to glory and *then* experience fullness of life. No! He promised us the abundant life that is the foretaste of glory *here and now*.

The fruit of the Spirit

"But the fruit of the Spirit is love, joy, peace, patience, kindness, goodness, faithfulness, gentleness and self-control. Against such things there is no law" (Galatians 5:22–23 NIV). Such fruit is the evidence of a life under God's control and in perspective. The apostle Paul was able to rejoice even in prison because of it. Our circumstances don't determine our outlook, but rather our perspective. Can you imagine a guy in prison (Paul, writing to the Galatians) telling people on the outside to lighten up?

When I was growing up, my brothers and I had daily chores to do. I could handle most of them, but one particular chore always got to me. I would do almost anything to get out of it: *doing the dishes*. My mom and dad made sure I finished the task and did it correctly, but I didn't like it and resisted it every time.

I'm not sure why I've always been so averse to that chore, but to this day I hate doing the dishes. Now I'm married, however. And on occasion (notice I didn't say "regularly"), I help my wife, Susan, by doing the dishes.

So what's the difference? Why will I do the dishes more willingly now?

Perspective.

The scenery is different (my wife compared to my mom). The rewards are different, too!

The circumstances haven't changed. The dishes are still filthy and slimy. But my perspective has changed. A life lived under the control of the Holy Spirit gives me perspective in the midst of a variety of circumstances.

God's promised blessings

Obedience always brings blessing. It's a basic principle of life that's deeply rooted in the Scriptures. Consider a few examples.

Israel was admonished, "O Israel, you should listen and be careful to do it, that it may be well with you and that you may multiply greatly, just as the Lord, the God of your fathers, has promised you, in a land flowing with milk and honey" (Deuteronomy 6:3 NASB).

We see another example in the Old Testament when the prophet Samuel confronted and counseled the self-seeking King Saul: "Samuel said, 'Has the Lord as much delight in burnt offerings and sacrifices as in obeying the voice of the Lord? Behold, to obey is better than sacrifice, and to heed than the fat of rams'" (1 Samuel 15:22 NASB).

Abram, who became Abraham, would never have become the father of a great nation had he not understood the blessing: "By faith Abraham, when he was called, obeyed by going out to a place which he was to receive for an inheritance; and he went out, not knowing where he was going" (Hebrews 11:8 NASB).

Consistency in life

Stability! I can't think of anything much worse than being in a small boat in a big sea with large waves. Life doesn't have to feel that way, however. Noah was a wonderful example of a man who didn't allow life to overwhelm him. In a time of great wickedness on the earth, he remained constant in his devotion to God, working for 120 years to build an ark according to God's command.

Or what about the psalmist in Psalm 1? His image of a tree planted by a source of nourishment so the roots can go down deep and withstand the storms of life is a wonderful picture of consistency.

Integrity

Integrity means that what's on the outside is a reflection of what's inside; it's the real substance of a man. Daniel illustrates this quality beautifully. When an order went forth that people were only allowed to pray in the name of Babylon's King Darius (Daniel 6), Daniel went to his upstairs room, where the windows were open, got down on his knees, and prayed to the God of heaven three times a day—"as he had been doing previously" (Daniel 6:10 NASB). There was no false show, but rather the simple living out of what was on the inside. It's interesting to note that not one negative thing is said about him in Scripture.

Deeper relationships

When we pursue the spiritual disciplines, we can also enjoy deeper relationships with God and with family, friends, and coworkers. The intimacy King David had with God is seen throughout the many psalms he wrote and in the fact that there's more written about him in the Scriptures than there is about anyone else besides Jesus. On a couple of occasions, God even called him a man after His own heart.

Stronger thought life

The Bible, through the apostle Paul, calls us to "take captive" every thought to the glory of Christ: "We are destroying speculations and every lofty thing raised up against the knowledge of God, and we are taking every thought captive to the obedience of Christ" (2 Corinthians 10:5 NASB).

The majority of the Christian men I know don't face serious struggles over what they *do* in their lives. Whether it's from positive peer pressure or fear of the consequences of sin, they control their actions most of the time. But those same men will tell you that controlling their *thought life* is quite another matter.

I once spoke at a conference in the Midwest where I was called upon to lead in a time of prayer. "Men," I announced, "if you have something you need to confess and deal with publicly, I want you to feel free to do so. We'll pray for you and any others with the same need."

No sooner had I finished the announcement than I observed a man rising to his feet to make a confession. "I have a problem with pornography," he said.

I looked around the room to observe the reaction from the other men. Rather than a sea of shocked faces, I saw many men lowering their heads, looking painfully at the ground.

"I don't buy it anymore," the man continued. "Actually, I haven't bought any since I was in college years ago. But my thought life is controlling me, and if I don't get control of it, it's only a matter of time before it will take over my actions. I want to be clean, and I want to be strong from the inside out. I don't want to patch up the outside so that no one will think I have a problem. I need to do more than that. I need help."

After he finished, a number of other men stood to confess the same struggle. It was one of the greatest prayer meetings I've ever been in. And as we develop the heart of a godly man, God will enable us to take captive our thoughts.

Another couple of verses to consider on this subject are found in Philippians:

> *And the peace of God, which surpasses all comprehension, will guard your hearts and your minds in Christ Jesus. Finally, brethren, whatever is true, whatever is honorable, whatever is*

right, whatever is pure, whatever is lovely, whatever is of good repute, if there is any excellence and if anything worthy of praise, dwell on these things. (Philippians 4:7–8 NASB).

Improved business life

Pursuing the spiritual disciplines can also improve our business lives. By that I mean that they can give us a moral compass that enables us to navigate the treacherous waters so often present in our business situations.

A few years ago, I was introduced to a businessman who had recently come to faith in Jesus Christ. In one of our many subsequent conversations, he asked me what the Bible had to say about business. I gave him a few passages to look up later that dealt with honesty, ethics, and fairness. I also offered to connect him with a couple of other Christian businessmen I knew in the area.

When I mentioned their names, I noticed his face took on a strange expression. "Glenn, don't bother," he said, looking disappointed.

"Why?" I asked.

"Well, even before I knew Christ, I had integrity in business. My word was my bond. I never backed down on a promise. I tried to treat my employees fairly. But I've got to tell you, Glenn, I've had dealings with the guys you just mentioned, and I don't see Christianity in their business practices. I'm sorry to say it, but it's the truth."

Those were strong words that told me those men were not growing spiritually. As we draw closer to Christ, it doesn't mean everything will forever after be great—we'll never lose a job, our bosses will always appreciate us, our companies will consistently be profitable, and so on. But we'll know what we're doing and why we're doing it. We'll have the moral compass necessary to navigate in a world filled with a variety of obstacles.

Character

The spiritual disciplines can produce character as well. Character means many things, but one thing included in its definition is that we can be trusted.

Several years ago, my family accompanied me to a Promise Keepers conference at the Georgia Dome in Atlanta. My wife was with some of the staff families in a skybox, while I was busy in meetings. My son, Justin, was out exploring the stadium with some of the other staff kids.

About halfway through the conference, a boy ran up to my wife to give her some news. "Mrs. Wagner, Justin is selling Cokes at one of the concession stands!" he declared.

Since Justin was only eleven years old at the time, Susan decided she needed to check this out. Sure enough, she discovered her boy working a concession stand! A long line of men was waiting to be served by Justin. He took their three dollars, passed them a Coke, and moved on to the next person in line. The money went into a cash box behind the counter, and to all who observed him, Justin looked like a pro.

Susan found a nearby security guard. "Excuse me, sir," she said. "Is this booth being run by the stadium or by Promise Keepers?"

"That's a stadium operation, lady," he replied.

"Do you think they want an eleven-year-old boy running it?" she asked calmly.

"I guess I'd better check into it," he responded.

Before long, the booth was closed down, much to the disappointment of the men who went without Cokes. They booed the guard but cheered for Justin as he exited the booth, thanking him for his service.

Justin smiled and said, "That was pretty cool, Mom!"

"Great. I'm glad you enjoyed it," she answered soberly. "By the way, you're grounded until you're thirty."

The next day, while we were still in the Georgia Dome, the security guard found Susan and me. "The management of the stadium gave me a message to give you about your son," he said.

We swallowed hard.

"They wanted me to pass on their commendation for your son's entrepreneurship!" he continued. "They also wanted you to know that they counted the number of cups sold, as well as the total cash in the box, and they matched perfectly!"

Now we were beaming proudly.

"The management wanted me to tell you that they haven't met a young boy with such character before."

"Did you just say my son is a character?" I asked.

"No, I said your son *has* character," he clarified.

We felt so proud! But now we were in a dilemma. Mom had grounded him, and the stadium management wanted to reward him!

I sat down with Justin and explained that he shouldn't have been so quick to jump behind the booth without first knowing who it belonged to. As soon as he was clear on that fact, I congratulated him, telling him how proud his mother and I were of his character. He had shown a desire to help out and that he could be trusted to do what's right.

That's what I want for his life. It's what I want for my life, too.

NO REGRETS

Growing up, like most kids I was involved in sports. I can still recall some of the coaches using the well-worn phrase "Remember, it's not whether you win or lose but how you play the game that counts." I never really believed that statement. I didn't think the coaches believed it, either; it was just a way to encourage the troops after a disappointing loss. Nor did some of the parents believe it. They held to the Vince Lombardi philosophy: "Winning isn't everything; it's the only thing."

The desire to win and be successful seems to be deeply ingrained in our psyches. Losing is tough. It's painful. It's embarrassing.

My senior year of high school, our football team played the squad from a much larger school. They had a greater number of students to draw from, and we knew going into the game that we were outnumbered. They had two or three guys to substitute for each position, whereas many of our guys had to play both ways. We were out-sized, out-coached, out-uniformed, and out-cheered by their massive throng of fans.

At halftime, we were already hopelessly behind in the score.

We sat in the locker room bruised, bleeding, broken, and bemoaning the fact that we still had another half to play. Our guys were dropping like flies, requiring that some of us play positions we had never played before. As the coach came in for his pep talk, I couldn't help but wonder what sort of "win one for the Gipper" speech he could pull out of his bag of tricks. We certainly needed something to motivate us.

He chose to give a speech I had heard before. This time, however, it really sunk in.

"Men, when you leave the field at the end of the fourth quarter, I want you to be able to walk off with no regrets," he said. "Give it your all, regardless of what the scoreboard says. I want you to be able to leave with your pride intact. Winners are those who give it their best. Now let's go out there and do it!"

I left the locker room shaking my head. *Be a winner by giving my best?* I thought. *Leave the field with pride? I just want to leave the field under my own power instead of in a body bag!*

But by the time I got to the field, I couldn't get the words "no regrets" out of my head. I've thought of that phrase so many times since that day as well. (As you can see, I have no intention of telling you the outcome of the football game.)

What am I playing the game of life for? *Who* am I playing it for? What does it mean to be a winner? If God should grant me a few moments of lucidity at the end of my life, will I be able to look back with a sense of satisfaction and fulfillment? I'm not saying I never messed up. I'm not saying I've never been carried off the field, or that I've never made stupid mistakes.

I'm not asking for a perfect life. But how about a life with no regrets?

Several years ago, I was hospitalized for something that ended up being not very serious. But for a few moments, we weren't sure what was going on. I can still remember Susan bringing our daughter, Haven, and our son, Justin, into the room to visit me. Justin was only ten years old at the time, and the sight of his dad wired up to monitors and tubes coming out of everywhere was too much for him. He turned to his mom and asked, "Mom, is Daddy going to die?"

While she assured him I was fine, his words pierced deeply into my soul. Even with all the medication given to me, I was awake most of the night, mulling over his comment.

What if I had died? I thought. *What would I be remembered for? How would I be eulogized?* I kept thinking, *Would they remember me for the books I wrote and the places I traveled to in order to minister? Would they talk about the people I've preached to? Would my wife be able to stand and say that, like the apostle Paul, I had fought the good fight and kept the faith?* (see 2 Timothy 4:7–8)

Several things stand out to me when I think about Paul's words. First, Paul knew he had fought the good fight. Maybe not *every* battle was won, but the important battles were. He was able to recognize those fights that had eternal significance, and those are the ones he fought hard for Christ.

Second, Paul *finished* the race. It's easy to begin a long race but difficult to finish. I have a friend who will remind me from time to time, "Glenn, run the race." When he says that, he means that my responsibility is to run the *right* race. I've heard incredible stories about marathon runners who've become so enamored of the cheering crowds that they take a wrong turn and get disqualified.

The world and even the church are filled with screaming fans telling us which way to run and what race to get into. I need to know how to discern the *best* from the many good options I have, pursuing it all the way to the finish line.

Third, Paul kept the faith. He didn't allow the distractions of trials and changing circumstances to alter his course.

That night as I sat awake in my hospital bed, I concluded that those are the marks of a well-lived life. You can call it a successful life or being a winner or living a life of significance; to me the name doesn't matter all that much.

What does matter is that I come to the end of my life and know:

I fought the right battles.
I finished the right race.
I kept the true faith.

The crown is awarded to those who finish the well-lived life. They look to get God's perspective rather than that of man.

As we seek to define what it means to develop the heart of a godly man, my desire is to have God look down, put His arms around me, and say as He did to David centuries before:

Glenn, you are a man after My heart.

That will be success. There will be no regrets. That's the kind of life that has a positive impact on the world, that leaves a legacy for my family, my church, and my community.

There are many benefits to pursuing the godly life. As we move into our study of the individual disciplines, may God be pleased to grant us the desire of our hearts . . . a heart that is godly.

CHAPTER THREE

A HEART FOR THE BIBLE

In his book *Spiritual Intimacy*, Richard Mayhue fires our imaginations by asking us to pretend that a copy of the Bible has been keeping a diary all year of its activity. A few of the entries would read like the following:

January 15:   Been resting for a week. A few nights after the first of the year my owner opened me, but no more. Another New Year's resolution gone awry.

February 3:   Owner picked me up and rushed off to Sunday school.

February 23:   Cleaning day. Was dusted off and put back in place.

April 2:   A busy day. Owner had to present the lesson at a church society meeting. Quickly looked up a lot of references.

May 5:   In Grandma's lap again, a comfortable place.

May 9:   She let a tear fall on John 14:1–3.

May 10:   Grandma's gone. Back to my old place.

May 20:   Baby born. They wrote his name on one of my pages.

July 1:   Packed in a suitcase—off for a vacation.

July 20:   Still in suitcase. Almost everything else taken out.

July 25:   Home again. Quite a journey, though I don't see why I went.

August 16:   Cleaned again and put in a prominent place. The minister is to be here for dinner.

August 20:   Owner wrote Grandma's death in my family record. He left his extra pair of glasses between my pages.

December 31:   Owner just found his glasses. Wonder if he will make any resolutions about me for the New Year?[1]

How does that Bible's journal compare to the one your copy of the Scriptures would have kept over the last year? Many of us Christian men have tons of good intentions when it comes to reading the Bible, but for any number of reasons, we just don't get around to it consistently. I don't say this to generate guilt, either. I'm just admitting that there are plenty of us who have the identical struggles.

A HEART FOR THE BIBLE: WHY?

Do you love God's Word? One would think that every Christian man would answer in the affirmative. The Bible is our life, our strength, our joy.

Yet statistics indicate that only about 10 percent of Christians read their Bible every day. More fall into the category of "once in a while," while others only look at it when the pastor preaches from it on Sunday morning or they're faced with a major crisis.

A fair question, then, is why should we love the Scriptures? King David took on that very issue in some of the comments he penned in Psalm 119:

> *May your unfailing love come to me, O Lord, your salvation according to your promise; then I will answer the one who taunts me, for I trust in your word. Do not snatch the word of truth from my mouth, for I have put my hope in your laws. I will always obey your law, for ever and ever. I will walk about in freedom, for I have sought out your precepts. I will speak of your statutes before kings and will not be put to shame, for I delight in your commandments because I love them. I reach out my hands for your commandments, which I love, and I meditate on your decrees.* (Psalm 119:41–48 NIV)

If you're like me, your eye is drawn to this phrase in that powerful text: "I delight in your commandments because I love them." How can he use such intimate terms? The text offers some reasons why we should all love the Word of God, just as David did.

It proclaims God's mercies and salvation (Psalm 119:41)

According to the Scriptures, salvation comes from the Word of God. It is the incorruptible seed that lives and abides forever. But I believe the psalmist was going even further than that statement because of his reference to "may your unfailing love come to me." That's a common theme in the Bible, as seen in another psalm: "The Lord is gracious and compassionate, slow to anger and rich in love. The Lord is good to all; he has compassion on all he has made" (Psalm 145:8–9 NIV).

I meet Christians all the time who view God as the deity sitting up in heaven holding a baseball bat, ready to club them for every false move they make. Throughout the Bible, however, we see that He is compassionate and good to all.

Every day is filled with the freshness of what God is going to do. He understands who we are and gives us grace rather than what we deserve. Whatever happens in our lives—from overflowing toilets to traffic jams to credit cards over their limit—it's good to remind ourselves that God is so good. By dwelling on that thought, He will often keep us from getting into more trouble. What a wonderful reason to love the Word of God—to simply learn more of His mercy and salvation!

It provides answers to all who reproach us (Psalm 119:42)

It's not easy to answer the questions that fill our world today. But the Bible prepares us and gives us the responses we need. David put it this way: "I will answer the one who taunts me, for I trust in your word."

When others taunt us, they mock us. They put us down because of our faith. This verse teaches that we will be able to answer them because of our trust in God's Word. This Old Testament passage is a great deal like Peter's words in the New Testament:

> *Who is going to harm you if you are eager to do good? But even if you should suffer for what is right, you are blessed. "Do not fear what they fear; do not be frightened." But in your hearts set apart Christ as Lord. Always be prepared to give an answer to everyone who asks you to give the reason for the hope that you have. But do this with gentleness and respect, keeping a clear conscience, so that those who speak maliciously against your good behavior in Christ may be ashamed of their slander. It is better, if it is God's will, to suffer for doing good than for doing evil.* (1 Peter 3:13–17 NIV)

Our understanding of God's Book will prepare us. Without it, we're out there all alone, without the right words to deal with those who need answers. His Word will also give us the gentleness we need to respond lovingly when others deal with us harshly or vindictively.

When life goes along just fine, we tend to forget how important it is to have answers. Sometimes it takes the entrance of a person who rips us up one side and down the other, blasting our Christianity, for us to see the value of the Word and the answers it offers.

It provides assurance (Psalm 119:43)

The Word is truth. Without it, we're like a ship without a rudder, tossed to and fro with every little problem that comes along. Our circumstances and the accompanying emotions can fill us with fear and doubt. Our confidence must be in the Lord and His truth.

I talk with so many guys who have lost their hope and confidence for any number of reasons. This always grieves me, for I know the Bible has the answers that would help restore their assurance. You see, the assurance of God's love and work in our lives doesn't come from our performance—it comes from His promises!

David said in verse 43, "Do not snatch the word of truth from my mouth, for I have put my hope in your laws." If you're a true believer, when you read the Bible, the Holy Spirit who lives in you (and who is the Author of the Book) bears witness with your spirit that what you're reading is the truth. If you're not a believer, Scripture can look like foolishness, because the natural man cannot discern spiritual things.

How sad that some of us would stumble along in our Christian lives, allowing circumstances to affect our confidence in the Lord, when we have a Book that we can read to gain assurance for our discouraged hearts!

It promises freedom (Psalm 119:45)

The most tied-up Christians I know are those who either ignore God's Word or misuse it. Perhaps they follow the opinions and traditions of men, or maybe they just talk a good talk, but they end up in bondage to themselves.

The good news, however, is that the Word sets us free! The apostle Paul told the Corinthians, "Now the Lord is the Spirit, and where the Spirit of the Lord is, there is freedom. And we, who with unveiled faces all reflect the Lord's glory, are being transformed into his likeness with ever-increasing glory, which comes from the Lord, who is the Spirit" (2 Corinthians 3:17–18 NIV).

Where do we see the glory of the Lord? In the Word! As we are being transformed into His likeness, one of the results is liberty. This gets me very excited. The more we allow the glory of the Lord to saturate our minds and hearts through reading the Word, the more it sets us free to be all God wants us to be. Plus we receive all the joy we've ever wanted, the peace we love to have, and God's forgiveness as well.

These do not come by putting a veil over our faces, which in Paul's words symbolizes *indirect* access to God. Rather, we're able to go directly to the Word to experience His glorious freedom.

Jesus told the people in John 8:36 that the truth would set them free and that "if the Son sets you free, you will be free indeed." By spending time in the Bible, we're set free from wrong thinking, discouragement, a life filled with bitterness and resentment, wrong attitudes, and wrong actions.

The more we know the Word, the greater freedom we'll experience.

It promotes boldness (Psalm 119:46)

"I will speak of your statutes before kings and will not be put to shame." The opposite of shame is boldness. We have no cause for embarrassment about our beliefs, because the gospel is the power of God.

The more of the Bible that gets into our lives, the more boldness we'll have. We'll be able to speak to people we never thought we could. This is a good thought to meditate on before going to work on Monday mornings!

Once again, consider the words of the apostle Paul:

> For God did not give us a spirit of timidity, but a spirit of power, of love and of self-discipline. So do not be ashamed to testify about our Lord, or ashamed of me his prisoner. But join with me in suffering for the gospel, by the power of God, who has saved us and called us to a holy life—not because of

anything we have done but because of his own purpose and grace. This grace was given us in Christ Jesus before the beginning of time, but it has now been revealed through the appearing of our Savior, Christ Jesus, who has destroyed death and has brought life and immortality to light through the gospel. And of this gospel I was appointed a herald and an apostle and a teacher. That is why I am suffering as I am. Yet I am not ashamed, because I know whom I have believed, and am convinced that he is able to guard what I have entrusted to him for that day. (2 Timothy 1:7–12 NIV)

Does that declaration ring true in your life? Can you say, like Paul, that you're not ashamed of the gospel? He said he was convinced—he knew what God had said and trusted it completely. The Word of God promotes boldness.

So how does a guy get into his Bible? I can think of at least five practical ways to do it. Let's look at each of them in turn. If you're an old hand at this stuff, read the following sections as if you've never studied the Word before, and ask the Lord for the gift of freshness.

A HEART FOR BIBLE READING

The most basic aspect of spending time in the Scriptures is to simply read them. This is reading as you would read a novel, a biography, or a book from a Christian bookstore. It's reading for education, enlightenment, and enjoyment. This is the part of the journey where we allow God to speak to us ever so quietly through His Word.

For many men, this kind of reading is the key part of the important daily routine called a *quiet time.*

When we read the Bible, we're listening to God speak to us. Thus, it's a wonderful idea to do it consistently. Now, the last thing I want to do is throw guilt around. Reading the Word is a great way to focus our thoughts on spiritual things, however, so the more often we do it, the better.

If you're a morning person, try beginning each day with a

few minutes in your Bible. But if you're like me, early mornings aren't your best time, and there's nothing wrong with reading the Word after you've had a couple of cups of coffee to start your day, or even at night before retiring. Some guys spend their lunch hour with the Lord, others their afternoon coffee break. Find the time of day that works best for you, then go for it.

Also, it's not the end of the world if you don't read the Bible every day. I know so many guys who stop reading their Scriptures *completely* because they missed a day here and there. If you can only squeeze out two days a week with the Word, that's all right for now—do it! If you're like me, your schedule varies from week to week and month to month. You may be in a particularly busy period at present. Perhaps in a month or two a larger window of regular time will open up for you. But begin to read today. You'll find that the more you read it, the more you'll want to read it every day. It will become your delight.

Don't misunderstand: The needs of life cry out so loudly that daily reading should be our goal. But start where you are and move forward. Sometimes small steps are the best steps—just so we're going in the right direction.

In terms of the actual reading, many guys find it helpful to use a newer translation of the Scriptures. The advantages are many, but here are just two: You read the Word in a fresh voice, and you read it in a language closely related to the everyday language we use.

I use a different translation of the Bible every year in my reading schedule. My goal is to read through the Bible in that twelve-month period. It works out wonderfully for me. The key is finding what works best for *you.* Discover your own comfort zone in reading the Word, and then proceed.

A HEART FOR HEARING A SERMON

An often-neglected aspect of spending time in the Word is hearing it proclaimed by a pastor or Bible teacher. As a visually oriented society, we sometimes forget God can work through auditory means as well. When was the last time you used your ears to *listen* for the words of the Lord?

There are many different ways to hear sermons. The most obvious is the weekly ministry of your local pastor. Are you gaining insights into God and His Word through your attention to his sermons? I hear many men complain about their pastors' "dull" style, but perhaps the problem has more to do with the men's expectations. Try this next weekend: Go to church, sit in the pew, and ask God to teach you something through the worship service. Let's just see if the Lord will answer your simple and sincere prayer.

Besides listening to your pastor, you can hear good Bible teachers on cassette tapes. It's now possible to hear the great preachers of today, as well as those of yesterday. Then there's the whole arena of pastors on the radio.

Many of the preachers on tape and on the air are expositional in style, meaning they teach verse by verse through the books of the Bible. This can be very helpful in our busy schedules. I know men who have thirty to forty minutes of quiet time with God each weekday by listening to a favorite teacher on the radio or on tape while commuting between work and home.

One other practical suggestion is to use Scripture on tape. Rather than reading the Bible, we can listen as it's read to us. This is a fresh way to approach the Scriptures and another good tool for the busy commuter.

A HEART FOR BIBLE STUDY

A step beyond reading the Word is studying the Word. This is a more serious pursuit that leads to a fuller and deeper understanding. You will also find that there's nothing like the joy of personal discovery of biblical truth.

Many excellent books outline the basics of personal Bible study. But reduced to its simplest form, they consist of four questions a Bible student should ask of every text he reads:

1. What does it say?

Simple observation is the foundation of Bible study, yet it's the most easily overlooked aspect. Take your time considering and answering this question.

2. What does it mean?

If observing is the foundation, this question is the construction of the building. Answering it calls for you to place yourself in the writer's shoes and consider, "What did it mean to the writer?"

3. How does it fit in with other Scripture passages?

This is where you look at your building's "neighborhood"—the surrounding verses and related passages. It's extremely important that you understand the context of the passage you're studying.

4. What does it mean to me?

Finally you move into the building. An important rule of thumb in personal Bible study is that there's only one interpretation of a passage, but there can be many applications. Your application, however, must be true to the interpretation.

The process of answering those four questions is referred to as observation, interpretation, correlation, and application. All four steps are necessary. If you try to interpret the verse before you understand what it says, you'll often miss the most important truths. Likewise, if you observe and interpret without correlating, you may take a verse out of context, causing it to say something it was never intended to say. And if you do all the preliminary work but don't apply the passage to your life, you don't allow it to influence your life in the way God desires.

To study the Bible well, some tools will be quite helpful. These include:

- A notebook in which to record your findings
- A different translation from the one you're used to, for comparison

- An English dictionary
- A Bible dictionary
- A Bible handbook
- A Bible encyclopedia
- A Bible atlas
- A Bible concordance
- A book of biblical introduction

These tools will help you achieve a fuller understanding of the verses you study. Take care to use tools that are sound in their teaching. Your pastor can help you choose titles that are best in each category.

I often hear men minimizing their study habits by minimizing their intellects. This is so sad to me. It reminds me of a story I heard concerning a young seminary student who played basketball in a church league. Whenever he played in this one church gym, he would see the custodian sitting in the corner, reading, looking as if he were waiting for everyone to leave so he could lock up and go home.

One night the student's curiosity finally got to him. "What are you reading?" he inquired.

"The Bible," the old custodian replied, never looking up from his reading.

The student found the answer intriguing. "Which part?" he asked with a smile on his face.

"Revelation," said the man of few words.

Surprised by his answer, the student quipped, "Do you understand such a complex book?"

"Yup," the custodian answered, still glued to the pages of his Bible.

The student was fascinated by this point. "Well then, tell me, what does it teach us?"

The custodian put down his Bible, looked the student squarely in the eye, and gave the definitive two-syllable answer: "God wins."

Like that seminary student, we all need to realize that

every person has the ability to study, learn, and understand the Scriptures. The Holy Spirit living within us makes it possible.

For some of us, it's time to get serious about studying the Word of God. We've put it off long enough. We've made enough excuses. Consider the words of R. C. Sproul, who seems to have his finger on the pulse of many of today's men:

> *Here, then, is the real problem of our negligence. We fail in our duty to study God's Word not so much because it is difficult to understand, not so much because it is dull and boring, but because it is work. Our problem is not a lack of intelligence or a lack of passion. Our problem is that we are lazy.*[2]

A HEART FOR BIBLE MEMORIZATION

A fourth way to spend time with God's Word is to memorize it. King David said, "Your Word I have treasured in my heart, that I may not sin against You" (Psalm 119:11 NASB).

Memorizing Scripture sounds painful and laborious to some, but the truth is that God will honor our efforts to remember His Word. Countless times in my own life and in the lives of other men, a passage of Scripture has come to mind at precisely the right moment, and in doing so it literally "rescued" us from making a poor decision or yielding to a sinful temptation. No, memorizing is not a punishment; it's a privilege.

One writer describes the long-lasting benefits of memorizing the Word of God this way: A pertinent scriptural truth brought to your awareness by the Holy Spirit at just the right moment can be the weapon that makes the difference in a spiritual battle.[3]

So many men have told me they can't memorize Scripture because they don't have a good memory. I realize that abilities vary, but *every man has the ability to memorize*. In fact, I'll bet you've memorized a large amount of current and past information. For instance, it's a safe guess that you know the statistics of your favorite athletes and sports teams. And how about directions around your town?

The problem isn't so much that we lack the ability to memorize Scripture, but rather that we don't always see the importance of it. We commit to memory those things we value. (Could this explain why we might forget our wife's birthday and our wedding anniversary, but we remember Babe Ruth's lifetime batting average?)

I was never real good with the index-card method of memorizing verses, although many men find it helpful. They just write out a verse on a card and then read it over and over until it eventually becomes a part of their memory.

For me, the key to memorizing came with the discovery that I needed to memorize verses that helped me in an area of current need or spoke to an issue of priority in my life. Thus, the passages took on special meaning. Memorizing had a purpose; I wasn't just going through the motions of a pedantic exercise. The more I learned, the more I wanted to learn. My mind became like a computer!

My first real computer used a floppy disk that held a relatively small amount of information. Then someone gave me a ten megabyte hard disk to install. I thought I was in heaven because of the amount of information I could now store! But soon even the hard disk didn't hold enough for what I needed to be able to retrieve at a moment's notice.

From there I got a larger hard disk, then a faster computer, more power, and more disk space. That's the ticket—more speed and more power! I'm even beyond megabytes to gigabytes today. I can retrieve necessary information in a split second and then apply it to the work situation at hand.

The same principle is at work in memorizing Scripture. When the Word is stored in the mind—with its incredible power, capacity, and speed—the Holy Spirit can operate our "computer." With the "touch of a key," He can bring to the forefront of our minds the truth that's needed at the very instant the need arises.

One of my teachers in Bible college used to remind us often of the need for Bible memorization. "Remember," he would gently implore, "what's in the well is what comes up in the bucket. So, students, what are you putting into the well of your life?"

Perhaps if he were still teaching today, he would update that encouragement for his students: "Remember, what's in the computer comes out on the screen or the printer. If you put in dirty data, expect to get junk back!"

A HEART FOR BIBLE MEDITATION

Once God's Word has been heard, studied, read, and memorized, its truth becomes rooted in our lives through meditation. Christian meditation is not the emptying of our minds or staring at the flying toasters on a computer screen, but rather the active and constructive thinking on significant truths of the Scriptures and how they apply to the realities of one's own life.

Four things are mentioned in the Bible as being worthy of our meditation:

- The Scriptures (the most-often-mentioned object by far)
- Creation
- God's providence
- God's person and attributes

We're to meditate on that which is revealed to us in the Word or informed by the Word. Meditation is spending time thinking deeply about what the Scriptures are saying to us in practical terms. I laugh when people think of meditation as sitting silently in a rose garden with their legs crossed, breathing deeply, humming a mantra while contemplating their navels.

Donald Whitney has a much better grasp on the art of meditation:

True success is promised to those who meditate on God's Word, who think deeply on Scripture, not just at one time each day, but at moments throughout the day and night. They meditate so much that Scripture saturates their conversation. The fruit of their meditation is action. They do what they find written in God's Word and as a result God prospers their way and grants success to them. . . .

Most information, even biblical information, flows through our minds like water through a sieve. There's usually so much information coming in each day and it comes in so quickly that we retain very little. But when we meditate, the truth remains and percolates. We can smell its aroma more fully and taste it better. As it brews in our brain the insights come. The heart is heated by meditation, and cold truth is melted into passionate action.[4]

A HEART FOR THE BIBLE: A PROPER RESPONSE

Returning to our look at Psalm 119, if we truly love God's Word, we can expect to see at least three different responses flowing out of our lives: obedience, joy, and trust.

Obedience

In the heart of the text we observed earlier, we find this statement: *"I will always obey your law, for ever and ever"* (v. 44). People who love God's Word are dedicated to obeying Him. This theme rings true throughout the entire psalm:

I will obey your decrees; do not utterly forsake me. (v. 8 NIV)

Do good to your servant, and I will live; I will obey your word. (v. 17 NIV)

Teach me, O Lord, to follow your decrees; then I will keep them to the end. (v. 33 NIV)

In the night I remember your name, O Lord, and I will keep your law. (v. 55 NIV)

I will hasten and not delay to obey your commands. (v. 60 NIV)

I am a friend to all who fear you, to all who follow your precepts. (v. 63 NIV)

Though the arrogant have smeared me with lies, I keep your precepts with all my heart. (v. 69 NIV)

Your statutes are wonderful; therefore I obey them. (v. 129 NIV)

Men who love God will obey God. And it will be evident in the way they live.

Joy

In the first psalm, we're told that godly men will delight in the Word day and night, meditating on it constantly. That same theme is developed in Psalm 119:

I delight in your decrees; I will not neglect your word. (v. 16 NIV)

Your statutes are my delight; they are my counselors. (v. 24 NIV)

Their hearts are callous and unfeeling, but I delight in your law. (v. 70 NIV)

Let your compassion come to me that I may live, for your law is my delight. (v. 77 NIV)

Because I love your commands more than gold, more than pure gold. (v. 127 NIV)

Men who have a heart for the Bible delight in it. Nothing is more important to them, and, as a result, it brings them great joy.

Trust

Loving the Word teaches us to depend on what it says: *"I reach out my hands for your commandments, which I love, and I meditate on your decrees"* (Psalm 119:48 NIV).

Lifting up one's hands is a powerful symbol of complete dependence on the Lord. It illustrates a man who trusts God with his life. The palms are open, not clenched. The fingers are pointing upward, indicating that all that comes to us in life comes from the Lord. The more I learn about God from His Word, the more I want to trust Him.

Do you love God's Word? If so, demonstrate that love by cultivating this all-important spiritual discipline of spending time in it.

J. I. Packer wrote insightfully about an effective strategy of Satan concerning our relationship with our Bible:

> If I were the devil, one of my first aims would be to stop folk from digging into the Bible. Knowing that it is the Word of God, teaching men to know and love and serve the God of the Word, I should do all I could to surround it with the spiritual equivalent of pits, thorn hedges, and man traps, to frighten people off. . . . At all costs I should want to keep them from using their minds in a disciplined way to get the measure of its message.[5]

Let's set a course to avoid those traps!

CHAPTER FOUR
A HEART FOR PRAYER

I t's a television program I will never forget.

I don't even remember the speaker's name, but I remember the couple of minutes I saw of him while channel surfing one afternoon. My trusty remote control in hand, I was zipping through all the channels when I stumbled upon a televised church service. I don't normally watch church on television, but I was fascinated by the fact that the preacher had a phone sitting on his pulpit. *Why would this guy have a phone by his side?* I thought. I was about to receive my answer.

"I want to talk with you today about the topic of prayer," the pastor began softly.

I still didn't get the connection with the phone.

"Prayer is just another way of saying we have a conversation with the Lord," he continued. "When is the last time you spoke with the Lord?"

Fortunately for my conscience, I had just talked with the Lord a short time before, so I didn't need to feel guilty.

"I've heard people say they don't talk to God because they're just too shy to approach Him. Well, I can understand your feelings. But I want you to understand a couple of important points.

First, God is always accessible. You need not feel intimidated approaching Him. As a matter of fact, He *wants* to talk with you. Second, even the shyest people I know have no problem talking on the phone. They can pick up the receiver and talk to their friends for hours."

With that, he picked up the phone and held it out toward the camera. "God is your friend. He wants to talk with you. Why don't you pick up your phone and talk with Him right now?"

Now, I confess, it was a little corny, but the image stuck with me. This guy had prayer nailed down tight. When we sweep away all the spiritual-sounding jargon, prayer is the wonderful privilege of carrying on an extended conversation with the living Lord.

Prayer is one of the most enjoyable spiritual disciplines. Men often neglect it, however, and the reasons are difficult to identify. To say it's due to a lack of training is an oversimplification. Prayer is not simply a ritual that happens at a prescribed time and precise place using a predetermined format.

Through prayer, God leaves the pages of history and is experienced as a present reality. He's more than just Jesus the historical hero. He is Someone we talk to in the current moment!

Let's take a closer look at how to make talking with God a more practical and accessible part of our lives. We'll begin by considering the benefits of prayer.

THE BENEFITS OF PRAYER

Why should we pray? Are there advantages? The Scriptures list dozens of benefits related to our prayer life. Consider just a few:

Peace of mind

"Be anxious for nothing, but in everything by prayer and supplication with thanksgiving let your requests be made known to God. And the peace of God, which surpasses all comprehension, will guard your hearts and your minds in Christ Jesus" (Philippians 4:6–7 NASB).

Purity of heart

"Be gracious to me, O God, according to Your lovingkindness; according to the greatness of Your compassion blot out my transgressions. Wash me thoroughly from my iniquity and cleanse me from my sin. . . . Purify me with hyssop, and I shall be clean; wash me, and I shall be whiter than snow." (Psalm 51:1–2, 7 NASB)

Power for service

"Now to Him who is able to do exceeding abundantly beyond all that we ask or think, according to the power that works within us, to Him be the glory in the church and in Christ Jesus to all generations forever and ever. Amen" (Ephesians 3:20–21 NASB).

Purpose in life

"Trust in the Lord and do good; dwell in the land and cultivate faithfulness. Delight yourself in the Lord; and He will give you the desires of your heart. Commit your way to the Lord, trust also in Him, and He will do it" (Psalm 37:3–5 NASB).

Presence of joy

"You will make known to me the path of life; in Your presence is fulness of joy; in Your right hand there are pleasures forever" (Psalm 16:11 NASB).

Prevention of temptation

"Keep watching and praying that you may not enter into temptation; the spirit is willing, but the flesh is weak" (Matthew 26:41 NASB).

That's a pretty amazing list of benefits, isn't it? It's hard to imagine that we not only have the privilege of talking directly to our heavenly Father, but He also rewards us with such an impressive list of positive results.

THE POWER IN PRAYER

A word that's always closely related to prayer is the word *power*. So much of what God can do in our world is directly related to the prayer life of believers like you and me. Consider some facts from Scripture:

Anyone can experience the power of prayer

"Therefore, confess your sins to one another, and pray for one another so that you may be healed. The effective prayer of a righteous man can accomplish much. Elijah was a man with a nature like ours, and he prayed earnestly that it might not rain, and it did not rain on the earth for three years and six months. Then he prayed again, and the sky poured rain and the earth produced its fruit" (James 5:16–18 NASB).

There's no limit to what God can do or how He does it

"For this reason, I bow my knees before the Father. . . . Now to Him who is able to do exceeding abundantly beyond all that we ask or think, according to the power that works within us" (Ephesians 3:14, 20 NASB).

The problem lies in our faith in God's power

"And Jesus answered and said to them, 'Truly I say to you, if you have faith and do not doubt, you will not only do what was done to the fig tree, but even if you say to this mountain, "Be taken up and cast into the sea," it will happen. And all things you ask in prayer, believing, you will receive'" (Matthew 21:21–22 NASB).

Our motives govern God's response to our prayers

"Whatever you ask in My name, that will I do, so that the Father may be glorified in the Son. If you ask Me anything in My name, I will do it" (John 14:13–14 NASB).

There's awesome power in prayer. The only weak link is our faith. We just don't realize how much God could do if we were only to trust Him completely. Prayer is an effective way of releasing much of our struggle, turning instead to His almighty power as our source of strength.

Be aware, however, that the Scriptures also warn about problems that will hinder our prayer life. Have you experienced any of these barriers in your prayer life?

THE BARRIERS TO PRAYER
Indifference to the Bible

"He who turns away his ear from listening to the law, even his prayer is an abomination" (Proverbs 28:9 NASB).

Sin that we refuse to give up

"If I regard wickedness in my heart, the Lord will not hear" (Psalm 66:18 NASB).

Marital conflict

"You husbands likewise, live with your wives in an understanding way, as with a weaker vessel, since she is a woman, and grant her honor as a fellow heir of the grace of life, so that your prayers will not be hindered" (1 Peter 3:7 NASB).

Inability to forgive others

"For if you forgive others for their transgressions, your heavenly Father will also forgive you. But if you do not forgive others, then your Father will not forgive your transgressions" (Matthew 6:14–15 NASB).

If you're like me, it takes the constant examination of your heart to be certain none of those barriers exist between you and the Lord. So let's go a step further. What sort of setting should we seek to create in order to have our prayers be most effective? The Bible speaks to this question as well.

THE CONTEXT FOR PRAYER
Faith

"And without faith it is impossible to please Him, for he who comes to God must believe that He is and that He is a rewarder of those who seek Him" (Hebrews 11:6 NASB).

Obedience

"And whatever we ask we receive from Him, because we keep His commandments and do the things that are pleasing in His sight" (1 John 3:22 NASB).

Thanksgiving

"Be anxious for nothing, but in everything by prayer and supplication with thanksgiving let your requests be made known to God" (Philippians 4:6 NASB).

Patience

"Yet those who wait for the Lord will gain new strength; they will mount up with wings like eagles, they will run and not get tired, they will walk and not become weary" (Isaiah 40:31 NASB).

Persistence

So I say to you, ask, and it will be given to you; seek, and you will find; knock, and it will be opened to you. For everyone who asks, receives; and he who seeks, finds; and to him who knocks, it will be opened" (Luke 11:9–10 NASB).

Humility

"Humble yourselves in the presence of the Lord, and He will exalt you" (James 4:10 NASB).

Don't let that list intimidate you. All of us fall short in some of those qualities. They represent prayer at its maximum effectiveness. It's still possible to have a strong prayer life without being perfect in every area.

I find great encouragement in John Gardner's words:

The primary function of prayer is not to act as a tool to control the forces that be, but it is rather a means of access whereby the disturbed and needy soul may come boldly into the presence of

God for the needed strength and courage to bear his load.[1]

THE TYPES OF PRAYER

We find a variety of prayers offered up in God's Word. Observing them gives us clear examples of the types of prayer we can use.

Here are four types:

Strength for self and other believers

"For this reason also, since the day we heard of it, we have not ceased to pray for you and to ask that you may be filled with the knowledge of His will in all spiritual wisdom and understanding, so that you may walk in a manner worthy of the Lord, to please Him in all respects, bearing fruit in every good work and increasing in the knowledge of God; strengthened with all power, according to His glorious might, for the attaining of all steadfastness and patience; joyously giving thanks to the Father, who has qualified us to share in the inheritance of the saints in Light" (Colossians 1:9–12 NASB).

Salvation of others

"Brethren, my heart's desire and my prayer to God for them is for their salvation" (Romans 10:1 NASB).

Supply of physical and material needs

"And my God will supply all your needs according to His riches in glory in Christ Jesus" (Philippians 4:19 NASB).

Workers for the harvest

"Seeing the people, He felt compassion for them, because they were distressed and dispirited like sheep without a shepherd. Then He said to His disciples, 'The harvest is plentiful, but the workers are few. Therefore beseech the Lord of the harvest to send out workers into His harvest'" (Matthew 9:36–38 NASB).

Those are specific types of prayers recorded in Scripture, but prayer isn't limited to those categories. We're able to offer up *everything* to the Lord, and He will hear us.

THE KEY TO EFFECTIVE PRAYER

The key to effective prayer is discussed in two separate passages written by the apostle John. Consider these words:

Whatever you ask in My name, that will I do, so that the Father may be glorified in the Son. If you ask Me anything in My name, I will do it. (John 14:13–14 NASB)

This is the confidence which we have before Him, that, if we ask anything according to His will, He hears us. And if we know that He hears us in whatever we ask, we know that we have the requests which we have asked from Him. (1 John 5:14–15 NASB)

If we were to sum up those verses in one succinct statement, it would be this:

Prayer is most effective when it's in the name of Jesus, according to the will of God.

This is not a magical formula or incantation. But praying in Jesus' name implies and should denote the spirit in which the prayer is offered. For prayer to be effective, we must pay the price to know the mind and spirit of Christ and then pray accordingly.

If our requests are in God's will, we'll always receive what we asked for. Often men say, "Why do we even have to ask God for things, since He already knows our needs?"

The best answer I can offer is to return to the illustration of a marriage. When I come home to Susan after a rough day at the office, she intuitively knows I've had a bad day as soon as I drag my weary body through the front door. But intimacy is developed between us when I "invite her in" to my world by talking about what took place. The sharing, the emotions, and the communication all add up to an important result. It's no longer just my day; it's *our day*. It's not just about me; it's about us.

It works the same way with God. He delights in hearing us recount the highs and lows of our day. It draws us closer to our Father. We develop even greater intimacy by opening up to Him.

Prayer really works. It will make a difference in your life. I can guarantee it because God guarantees it.

THE ASPECTS OF PRAYER

So how do I structure my prayers? Through the centuries, prayer has been approached in many ways. Some approaches have seemed overly simplistic, and others have been so complex that it's nearly impossible for the average guy to figure them out.

I first discovered a helpful method many years ago that's simple and has been a good model for my personal prayer life ever since. It uses the word *ACTS* as an acronym:

A = *Adoration*

Begin your prayer with praise for the Lord. Thank Him for His greatness. Spend a few minutes communicating to Him how much you love Him. Isn't it amazing that He is so great, yet so accessible?

C = *Confession*

The second aspect of prayer is cleansing yourself before Him. Admit to God your shortcomings, confess your sins, and ask for His forgiveness. This is a wonderfully therapeutic part of Christian prayer. The apostle John tells us that if we confess our sins, He will forgive them (see 1 John 1:9). The catharsis you feel from having your soul cleansed is like no other part of life.

T = *Thanksgiving*

The third part of prayer is fun! Think of all the things God has done for you, and give thanks for them. What needs has He met recently? How about needs He met for you in the last few years? What did He do for you when Jesus died on the cross? Thanksgiving can take place over all of history! I know so many guys who come away from prayer incredibly encouraged because they've spent so much time giving thanks for all their blessings. It can help put the problems of life into perspective.

S = *Supplication*

Finally, bring your requests to the Lord. For most of us, it's good to start by spending time with the first three aspects of prayer; otherwise, we're tempted to feel that prayer is only about asking for stuff. If your prayer life has been characterized by just "Gimme, gimme, gimme," you need to begin exploring those other aspects.

The ACTS list is not some legalistic chart to be checked off upon completion. It's merely a guideline that has helped me develop a more balanced prayer life. With this list, I can make a quick review and see if I'm covering all the areas.

Prayer can take place in a variety of settings. I know guys who have a healthy prayer life that takes place during their morning commute. I know others who enjoy talking to God while taking an extended jog. The point is that prayer can be approached creatively and with great flexibility.

A friend of mine has a kneeling bench that he visits regularly. I like that because it's a specific place where he goes to meet with the Lord. But, like any good thing, it can be made bad if it's set up as a standard we must all follow. Don't go out and buy a kneeling bench just because someone else uses one. Find what works best for you, and stick with it.

It's the same with the idea of the "prayer closet." If you have a place where you can be alone with God, that's great. But the Lord hears the man who prays silently in the middle of the Amtrak local from Arlington Heights to Chicago just as well as He hears the guy all alone in his closet. That's the great thing about the Lord—He's always available, always accessible.

During my first pastorate, I met a woman who radically changed the way I think about prayer. I remember I was sitting in a prayer circle with a half dozen folks when this woman of middle age took her turn to pray. There was nothing noticeably different about her appearance. She was a nice lady, like your mother, wife, or sister. But when she opened her mouth to pray, my opinion of her changed. Her voice was soft, but I felt strongly that she was *talking to God*. It was so personal, so warm, and so familiar that I thought that if I had opened my eyes, I would see Jesus sitting right next to her.

It was like a wonderfully intimate conversation two people would have over the dinner table. Two old friends were connecting on the issues of the day, both big and small. I left that prayer meeting a changed man, for I had learned a simple but vital lesson about prayer . . .

It's all about one heart connecting with another.

CHAPTER FIVE

A HEART FOR WORSHIP

W hat do you think of when you see the word *worship?* Does it conjure up a mental picture of a gothic cathedral, complete with pipe organ, robed choir, candles, and pews? Or do you see a quiet spot up in the mountains, perhaps sitting on a rock by a fast-moving stream, enjoying the silence as a time of reflection and rejuvenation? Maybe you see yourself in the middle of a contemporary Christian concert, the praise band leading the entire audience in a chorus of joyful singing. Or perhaps it's none of those pictures, just something more routine like sitting quietly at your dining room table with your Bible and a hot cup of coffee on an early winter's morning.

Well, if any of those mental images sounded like worship to you, there's good news: The correct answer is (e) all of the above.

The word *worship* is used by Christians for a wide variety of meetings, gatherings, activities, and actions. For instance, several months ago, I was preaching in a southern church. As I sat on the platform, the pastor made a variety of announcements and remarks. He finished by saying, "We are very happy to have Dr. Wagner with us this morning to lead our worship service."

A flood of thoughts passed through my mind as I considered that phrase, including the frightening thought that he expected me to lead the congregation in singing! Everyone who knows me well knows that while I love to sing praise to the Lord, the quality of my voice leaves much to be desired.

Fortunately for both me and the congregation, the pastor only expected me to preach. While I think he misused the term *worship,* for worship should involve *all* that's taking place, not just the message, each of us has his confusing preconceptions.

Richard Mayhue put worship in a wonderful perspective when he wrote, "Worship involves the highest privilege and the most exalted of experiences. It is the apex of Christian living. Worship fuels intimacy with God and heightens our commitment to God's kingdom purpose."[1]

If Mayhue's words ring true in your heart, as they do in mine, it's worthwhile to do a deeper investigation into the many forms of worship. Of all the definitions of worship I've found, and even tried to write, I don't think I've found one more clear and concise than the one Warren Wiersbe offers: "Worship is a believer's response of all that he is—mind, emotions, and body—to all that God is and says and does."[2]

Earlier in the same book, Wiersbe gave these honest insights:

> *When you consider all the words used for worship in both the Old and New Testaments, and when you put the meanings together, you find that worship involves both attitudes (awe, reverence, respect) and actions (bowing, praising, serving). It is both a subjective experience and an objective activity. Worship is not an unexpressed feeling, nor is it empty formality. True worship is balanced and involves the mind, the emotions, and the will. It must be intelligent, it must reach deep within and be motivated by love; and it must lead to obedient actions that glorify God.*[3]

In the Gospel of John, we see an important reference to worship in the earthly experience of Christ. Jesus had been involved in some intense ministry over a period of several months. It's hard work to preach, teach, travel, and spend time with a bunch of guys who just don't seem to get it. He had ministered to those who were hostile and to those who were jealous because their leader, John the Baptist, was decreasing in fame and influence, while Jesus was increasing, just as John had foretold. Plus there were the Pharisees who were so jealous that it was necessary for Jesus to leave Judea. Tired and perhaps a bit weary of heart, Jesus sat by Himself at Jacob's well (see John 4).

A Samaritan woman came to draw water. In spite of the racism of the day between Jews and Samaritans, Jesus asked this woman for a drink. A conversation then took place as she addressed the long-standing controversy between the Jews and Samaritans over the correct place to worship. Jesus cut past the issues of class, culture, race, and denomination to say, "God is spirit, and those who worship Him must worship in spirit and truth" (John 4:24 NASB).

In those words, He defined worship for us.

We'll come back to this passage later in this chapter. For now, however, note that true worship is always in accordance with truth and involves the inner being of a person (spirit), not just outward acts. Worship, in other words, involves the whole person.

WHY WORSHIP?

A. W. Tozer once said, "God wants worshippers before workers; indeed the only acceptable workers are those who have learned the lost art of worship. . . . The very stones would praise him if the need arose, and a thousand legions of angels would leap to do his will." [4]

Many of us have had the experience of trying to think of excuses that would get us out of worship on a Sunday morning. As a pastor, I think I've seen and heard them all. Here's one of my favorite letters:

Dear Pastor:
You often stress attendance at worship services as being important for a Christian, but I think a person has a right to miss now and then. I think every person ought to be excused for the

following reasons and the number of times indicated:

> *Christmas (Sunday before or after)*
> *New Year's (party lasted too long)*
> *Easter (get away for the holiday)*
> *July 4 (national holiday)*
> *Labor Day (need to get away)*
> *Memorial Day (visit hometown)*
> *Last day of school (kids need break)*
> *First day of school (one last fling)*
> *Family reunions (mine and wife's)*
> *Sleep late (Saturday night activities)*
> *Death in family*
> *Anniversary (second honeymoon)*
> *Sickness (one per family member)*
> *Business trips (a must)*
> *Vacation (three weeks)*
> *Bad weather (ice, snow, rain, clouds)*
> *Ball games*
> *Unexpected company (can't walk out)*
> *Time changes (spring ahead, fall back)*
> *Specials on TV (Super Bowl, etc.)*

Pastor, this leaves only two Sundays per year. So, you can count on us to be in church on the fourth Sunday in February and the third Sunday in August unless providentially hindered.

> *Sincerely,*
> *A Faithful Member*

If we spent the time worshiping that we do making excuses to get out of worship, we'd be the most spiritual nation in the world! But seriously, we do need to ask an important question.

Have you ever asked yourself why Christians gather together? In thousands of cities and towns around the world, Christians convene regularly and conduct a service of some sort. Usually it happens on Sunday, but more and more churches hold services on Fridays, Saturdays, and even midweek. The question is, however, why get together at all? In short, why worship, not only corporately, but also privately?

The Bible is filled with answers to this all-important question. And without the Scriptures, we're in danger of worshiping the God we want rather than the God who is. Let's consider a few of the most important teachings.

It's why God created us

Have you ever thought about why God made you? Why did He make the world? Why did He design it as He did? The Westminster Shorter Catechism says it well: "The chief end of man is to glorify God and enjoy Him forever."

The Scriptures tell us that everything was designed by God to worship and praise Him: "You alone are the Lord. You made the heavens, even the highest heavens, and all their starry host, the earth and all that is on it, the seas and all that is in them. You give life to everything, and the multitudes of heaven worship you" (Nehemiah 9:6 NIV).

Everything was made by God to point a finger back to Him, saying, "You alone are worthy." In the book of Revelation, we enter the throne room of God to hear:

And when the living creatures give glory and honor and thanks to Him who sits on the throne, to Him who lives forever and ever, the twenty-four elders will fall down before Him who sits on the throne, and will worship Him who lives forever and ever, and will cast their crowns before the throne, saying, "Worthy are You, our Lord and our God, to receive glory and honor and power; for You did create Your all things, and because of Your will they existed, and were created." (Revelation 4:9–11 NASB)

In heaven, we will fall down before God who sits on the throne and worship Him. It's the primary reason behind the creation of life and all things. It answers the age-old question of why we're here.

And I saw another angel flying in midheaven, having an eter-nal gospel to preach to those who live on the earth, and to every nation and tribe and tongue and people; and he said with a loud voice, "Fear God, and give Him glory, because the hour of His judgment has come; worship Him who made the heaven and the earth and sea and springs of waters." (Revelation 14:6–7 NASB)

Those are just two examples of a profound teaching in God's Word: We are to worship God because of His creation and what He has done. It's the key reason behind all He created. Our English word *worship* literally means "worth-ship." We are wor-shiping Him who is worthy—ascribing worth.

But there are other reasons we should worship as well.

It recognizes the holiness of God

We don't understand much about God's holiness today; worship is a profound realization of that holiness. The basic rea-son we don't worship more is that we don't truly understand God's character. The word *holiness* literally means "to be sepa-rate." When someone says God is holy, it means:

1. He is separate from everything evil.
2. He is separate from everything He has created.

Look more closely at that second statement. God is not on this page or in the pulpit. That would be pantheism. God is tran-scendent even though He is personal. He is separated from everything He has created, including the universe and the high-est heaven. The Lord is not to be confused or identified with what He has made. Those things merely express His greatness and attributes.

In the Old Testament, Moses was given the Ten Command-ments, and God made a fascinating statement concerning wor-ship and holiness: "Then he said to Moses, 'Come up to the Lord, you and Aaron, Nadab and Abihu, and seventy of the el-ders of Israel. You are to worship at a distance, but Moses alone is to approach the Lord; the others must not come near. And the people may not come up with him'" (Exodus 24:1 NIV).

One of the first references to worship in Scripture has God instructing people to worship from a distance. In this, we see the distinction between ourselves and God. Realizing who God is and who we are puts things in their proper perspective. It will eliminate pride and arrogance on our part. It stops us from demanding that God do things our way. Instead, we should fall before Him and seek His will, giving Him glory, worship, and praise.

> *Ascribe to the Lord, O families of the peoples, ascribe to the Lord glory and strength. Ascribe to the Lord the glory due His name; bring an offering, and come before Him; worship the Lord in holy array.* (1 Chronicles 16:28–29 NASB)

A generation ago, Archbishop William Temple made this insightful observation concerning worship: "To worship is to quicken the conscience by the holiness of God, to feed the mind with the truth of God, to purge the imagination by the beauty of God, to open the heart to the love of God, to devote the will to the purpose of God."[5]

Of course, this not only teaches us about God's holiness, but also about our need to approach Him with a clean heart. Donald Whitney wrote about the privilege of worshiping a holy God:

> *To worship God is to ascribe the proper worth to God, to magnify His worthiness of praise, or better, to approach and address God as He is worthy. . . . If you could see God at this moment, you would so utterly understand how worthy He is of worship that you would instinctively fall on your face and worship Him.*[6]

That's the kind of worship we read about all through the book of Revelation.

It's the proper response of a believer to God's goodness and salvation

"Man cannot live all to this world. If not religious, he will be superstitious. If he worships not the true God, he will have his idols."[7] Those words of Theodore Parker, written more than a hundred years ago, still ring true today.

There's a story told of a little, elderly woman who was part of the Salvation Army. She visited England late in her life to trace some of the roots of the Army. While on a tour of one of that country's magnificent cathedrals, she heard the tour guide say that the marvelous stained glass windows and glorious architecture provided the perfect atmosphere in which to worship God.

"I have a question," the woman interrupted when she felt she couldn't hold it in any longer.

"Yes?" the tour guide responded.

"How many people have come to believe in Jesus Christ as their Savior in this place?"

Clearly bothered by her question, the tour guide snapped back, "Madam, I am afraid you don't understand. This is a cathedral, not a chapel!"

Do you see the fallacy in that man's thinking? He had differentiated two concepts that go hand in hand. God has saved us; He's the Great Redeemer of our souls. That's precisely why we should worship Him! The Salvation Army woman was right on. Worship is the product of a heart that knows it has been set free. Now that it's forgiven, it can't resist—it just has to shout praises to the Lord in worship.

The children of Israel set an example for us to follow as they lived as slaves in Egypt: "So the people believed; and when they heard that the Lord was concerned about the sons of Israel and that He had seen their affliction, then they bowed low and worshiped" (Exodus 4:31 NASB). Seeing the goodness of God's grace and knowing He would deliver them, the people's only proper response was worship.

Ray Ortlund wrote:

Worship is the highest and noblest act that any person can do.

When men worship, God is satisfied! And when you worship, you are fulfilled! Think about this: why did Jesus Christ come? He came to make worshippers out of rebels. We who were once self-centered have to be completely changed so that we can shift our attention outside of ourselves and become able to worship him.[8]

Let's look at yet another reason we worship.

It's the natural result of those who know God's greatness and power

The more we know about our Lord, the more logical worship becomes. We just can't help it, for God is awesome! Oswald Chambers said it this way: "Worship is giving God the best He has given us!" King David understood God's greatness and power. He wrote:

All the ends of the earth will remember and turn to the Lord, and all the families of the nations will worship before You. For the kingdom is the Lord's, and He rules over the nations. All the prosperous of the earth will eat and worship, all those who go down to the dust will bow before Him, even he who cannot keep his soul alive. (Psalm 22:27–29 NASB)

The New Testament equivalent passage is found in Revelation:

And they sang the song of Moses, the bond-servant of God, and the song of the Lamb, saying, "Great and marvelous are Your works, O Lord God, the Almighty; righteous and true are Your ways, King of the nations. Who will not fear, O Lord, and glorify Your name? For You alone are holy; for all the nations will come and worship before You, for Your righteous acts have been revealed." (Revelation 15:3–4 NASB)

What a wonderful description of worship! It's people saying, "God, You are great! You're in charge. You will take over the world and judge everybody. All the nations will come to understand that fact, so we have only one natural response, and that is to worship You."

The great theologian C. S. Lewis had his finger on the relationship between God's glory and our worship when he wrote, "A man can no more diminish God's glory by refusing to worship him than a lunatic can put out the sun by scribbling the word darkness on the walls of his cell."[9]

It's more about what goes on inside than what's on the outside

Erwin Lutzer said well,

> *Worship isn't just listening to a sermon, appreciating the harmony of the choir, and joining in singing hymns! It isn't even prayer, for prayer can be the selfish expression of an unbroken spirit! Worship goes deeper. Since God is spirit, we fellowship with him with our spirit; that is, the immortal and invisible part of us meets with God, who is immortal and invisible.*[10]

As we saw earlier, Jesus Himself said in John 4 that worship must be in spirit and in truth. That's an incredible teaching. Christ was contrasting what goes on inside us with what we do on the outside. In a sense, that's the great conflict of worship. Our hearts may say one thing, but we act differently. Perhaps we can learn to rejoice outwardly, clap our hands, stand in praise to God, yell "Amen!" or whatever. But that isn't the key. The prime issue is what happens in the heart. As Richard Foster wrote, "If worship does not change us, it has not been worship. To stand before the Holy One of eternity is to change. Worship begins in holy expectancy; it ends in holy obedience."[11]

The externals aren't wrong if the internal is right. It's more a matter of focus. I believe when Jesus mentioned "spirit" in this passage, He was referring to our human spirit. It's that which is inside us that responds to God. And Jesus linked it intimately with the truth. To me, that speaks of *control*. Together, spirit and truth combine for biblical, Christ-centered worship.

Once again, consider the words of Donald Whitney:

How is it possible to worship God publicly once each week when we do not worship Him privately throughout the week? Can we expect the flames of our worship of God to burn brightly in public on the Lord's Day when they barely flicker for Him in secret on other days? Isn't it because we do not worship well in private that our corporate worship experience often dissatisfies us? . . . Focusing on the world more than on the Lord makes us more worldly than godly. But if we would be godly, we must focus on God. Godliness requires disciplined worship.[12]

In our worship, let's not fall into the trap of believing the *forms* can't change. A form is simply the shape in which a culture or generation of people express a feeling. The truth remains; the expression changes.

Worship is for all of us. Even though we've seen an impressive list of the whys and hows, it's enough to say that we worship because God wants us to.

I lay my "whys"
before your cross
in worship kneeling,
my mind too numb
for thought,
my heart beyond ·
all feeling;
And worshipping,
realize that I
in knowing You
don't need a "why."

Ruth Bell Graham[13]

CHAPTER SIX

A HEART FOR
SOLITUDE AND FASTING

I met Jake at a Promise Keepers event. To look at him, he would remind you of a thousand other guys. His brown hair neatly combed, six feet tall with a great smile, he was dressed in faded blue jeans, a scuffed-up pair of tennis shoes, and a stylish golf shirt. He could have been any one of us.

As we talked over two Styrofoam cups of steaming coffee, however, I realized Jake was different from many of us in at least one way. I quickly discovered he was one of those rare men honest enough to admit some of the spiritual issues with which he struggled.

After a bit of small talk, he felt safe with me, so he began to open up. "Glenn, I hear all the time about the importance of spending time alone with the Lord each day," he said. "You even spoke about it in your message today."

"You're right, Jake," I replied. "Some of the best times of each day can be those times alone with God."

"I guess so," he answered halfheartedly.

"You don't sound very excited about time alone with God," I suggested.

"I'm not," he said, looking away as if ashamed.

"Do you want to tell me about it?"

He looked troubled at this point. Taking his time, he took a deep breath before replying, "It's weird to say it out loud, but *I'd be afraid to be alone with God.*"

I've never forgotten Jake's words. I believe he represents a lot of men today. We like the comfort zone created by hanging around with familiar friends. If we're wired a certain way, we can remain superficial with those guys without fear of criticism. We don't ever have to worry about getting inside ourselves to see what's really going on. That's part of why being alone with God sounds scary.

Many men haven't been alone for years. They have surrounded themselves with others to provide a cushion. They may not be as free to admit it as Jake was, but the truth is, if they were asked to be alone, they'd be absolutely terrified.

Maybe you can identify with Jake; maybe not. Perhaps your concern is more like the one Lawrence raised to me at a discussion about the spiritual disciplines. Taking me aside in much the same way Jake did, Lawrence began, "Often after hearing a challenging message about spending time alone with God, I have a strong desire to carve out some time to do just that."

"That's great," I encouraged.

"*But,*" he continued, "then I start to think about how to fill the time. That's where I get confused."

"I can understand your confusion," I said.

"Tell me, Glenn," he asked sincerely, "what does a guy do when it's just him and God?"

Lawrence was speaking for men everywhere when he asked that question. Let's talk about the answer.

Ron DelBene gives a good response in his book *Alone with God: A Guide for Personal Retreats:* "Many of us find it extremely difficult to be alone with God because we are not sure what to do and have no idea what to expect. Uncertainty is not something we like to admit, but it does exist and is a barrier that anyone seriously concerned about personal spiritual growth must break through."[1]

Being alone with God can make anyone nervous. Extroverts dread the very thought of it because it calls them away from other people, and other people energize them. But it also presents a problem for introverts because it calls them away from themselves.

The spiritual discipline of solitude is one that can hit a guy like a surprise curveball early in the count. What's solitude all about, and how should one go about approaching it? Let's take a closer look.

A HEART FOR SOLITUDE

There's an old saying that silence is golden. To modernize it, my kids would say, "Silence is golden . . . not!" There's nothing worse than getting the silent treatment in our society.

Remember how bad it made you feel to be ignored in junior high? Knowing that everyone else was talking but you weren't included was pure torture.

Theoretically, we should have outgrown the silent treatment when we became adults. So much for theory. Adults can be the worst about using it. Unfortunately, one of the most common settings for this abuse is in a marriage, where we can wield it with great effectiveness against a spouse.

How about as a child? Were you ever sent to your room—no radio, no television, no talking, no singing—to just sit there in silence and think about what caused you to be sent there in the first place? In that case, silence became the enemy of your fun.

Others of us have been raised with the notion that being quiet means doing something sneaky or wrong. Remember when Mom would yell up to your room, "I can't hear you up there, so you must be doing something wrong"?

How about the silence of an awkward first date? You couldn't think of anything to say to keep the conversation going, so there were periods of painful quiet that even now make you cringe as you remember them.

All these sorts of influences from the past and present come into our thinking when we contemplate spending time alone with the Lord. Yet time alone with us is exactly what God desires. He wants to get to know us. I remember hearing someone say once that *love* is spelled T—I—M—E. Not bad theology.

Another important distinction to be made is the difference between being alone and being lonely. Loneliness is a difficult place to be, indeed. But being alone means placing ourselves in a setting where we're free from distraction and better able to focus on God. In this sense, being alone is a positive experience, for it's an opportunity to discover the depth within ourselves.

Being attentive is a key to being alone with God. We've all been in conversations, for example, where we knew the other person wasn't paying attention to us. Whether the distraction came from outside or inside the individual, we could see he or she wasn't with us mentally.

I can't tell you how many times I've been speaking to my children and have experienced this phenomenon (we'll leave my wife out of this one). Their eyes begin to wander in another direction. It's like trying to talk to a brick wall. Plenty of talk is happening, but little or no communication.

When they were small, I would often gently grab their little chins to get eye to eye with them. That way, I was able to "help" them pay attention.

Much of the same behavior occurs between us and the Lord. He's trying to communicate with us, but we allow our minds to wander. He must think we have the attention span of a gnat! And sadly, when we fail to pay attention, we often miss important details and opportunities.

So let's get specific. How do we make solitude—time alone with God—a part of our lives? If you're like me, you need a strategy. First, let's start small. Don't try to spend a whole day with the Lord until you've done parts of days. Second, let's minimize the fear and intimidation factor. The following are some practical suggestions.

Find a place

Where can you go to meet regularly with God? The number-one criterion for this place is that it must be as free from distraction as possible. It may be in the family room early in the morning before everyone else wakes up. It may be at your desk during the lunch hour. Perhaps it's in a lawn chair on the deck or during a long walk. It may be in your easy chair after everyone else has retired for the evening.

Why the emphasis on no distractions? When a child is diagnosed with attention deficit disorder (ADD), teachers are instructed to place the child's desk at the front of the classroom. This is not a punishment but rather helps the student pay attention without distraction from the other children. Makes sense, doesn't it?

Due to our sin nature, you and I suffer from spiritual ADD. We need to put ourselves in a place of few distractions so we can pay attention to what God is trying to say to us.

Set a time

We also need to set a regular time for meeting with God. The most important aspect of this is to choose one that works for you. For years, I tried to spend time with the Lord early in the morning, knowing full well I wasn't a morning person. It sounded so spiritual to give God those predawn hours, but I have no idea what God was trying to say in those early encounters, because I was too fried to pay attention.

For me, later in the morning works much better. I can pay attention then, and I'm more refreshed.

Set a time that works for you, and honor it.

Follow a plan

To make solitude work, most of us need a plan. The purpose of the plan is to protect us from some of the temptations we'll face. It's so easy to be drawn away from the Lord. Consider these issues that should be part of a practical plan for quiet time:

Protect the place. Make certain there are no phone interruptions. Turn off your pager. Refuse to answer the door. Do whatever it takes.

Protect the heart. This is where prayer comes into the picture. Ask the Lord to guard your heart from the distractions and temptations that can so easily lead you astray. If you need a refresher course on the incredible power and value of prayer, reread chapter 4.

Protect the mind. Reading Scripture will help you here. Something about reflecting on all God has done for us keeps our minds free from the distractions that can otherwise mess up the process.

Protect the memory. Learn the discipline of writing down what you hear God saying. What you've learned will become a valuable resource to you, not only right away but in the future as well, since you've taken the time to record it.

That leads us to another important aspect of solitude, the discipline of journaling.

A HEART FOR JOURNALING

In many circles, journaling is not considered a masculine thing to do. In fact, in an informal survey I conducted with a group of men, one man wrote this note: "Diaries are for girls." While diaries might be, I beg to differ when it comes to journaling. Recording your spiritual journey is not only a valuable tool for yourself, but think also of the spiritual legacy you'll pass on to your children. Reviewing God's work in your life can be incredibly encouraging.

Do you like to travel? Those who have the best recall of their trips always have two items at their disposal, a camera and a journal. The camera allows them to photograph the sights and scenery that will provide hours of enjoyment in the future. And the journal lets them record the places they visit, the exciting encounters, and the important memories of the trip.

It's the same principle for our spiritual journal.

Webster defines a journal as "an account of day-to-day events, a record of experiences, ideas, and reflections kept for private use." A spiritual journal is a record of our experiences of God in the events of the day, in the people we meet, but especially in our experiences of prayer. In addition, we can record these other facets of our daily lives:

- the status of interpersonal relationships
- daily routines, duties, work
- efforts on behalf of God's kingdom
- spiritual readings
- prayer efforts

Just as we learn from history in general, so also we learn from our personal history. We can reflect on our successes, failures, joys, and sorrows. Further, journaling can keep us accountable to be doers of the Word and not simply hearers. Journaling provides a reflective mirror in which we can learn to see ourselves more clearly. It forces us to be honest with ourselves and the Lord. It also makes us more appreciative of what the Lord has done and more responsive to His work in our lives.

David Rosage, in his book *Beginning Spiritual Direction,* offers practical counsel on getting started in journaling. First, purchase a notebook, spiral or bound, for your journal. Get something that won't fall apart.

Rosage also suggests trying one or both of two journaling methods. One he calls the awareness journal. This is not a diary or a listing of events and happenings of the day. Rather, it's an account of the important experiences that influence your spiritual journey. You also use this as a way to recount your relationship with the Lord and what He seems to be doing in your life. Rosage suggests the following questions to be asked during this process:

- Was I aware of the Lord's presence with me, or was I totally or partially oblivious to His love at every moment?
- Was I grateful for His gifts and graces, taking time to thank Him?
- Did I pause to listen to the Lord speaking to me today— through creation, through other people, and through my own thoughts?
- Did I take time to reflect on the thoughts the Lord brought into my mind?

- What was God's special gift to me today?

The second type of journal Rosage recommends is what he calls a prayer journal. In it you should list the day and date and then record where you prayed and the time you spent in prayer. This is not to produce guilt but motivation. Ask yourself the following questions, the answers to be recorded in your prayer journal:

- What happened in prayer?
- Was my prayer time peaceful? Quiet? Relaxed?
- Was I restless? Distracted? Worried? Anxious?
- Did the time pass quickly? Slowly?
- Did I get to know Jesus in a more personal way as I listened to Him?
- Did I grow closer to the Father?

Journaling is a wonderful way to converse with God. It helps me fight distractions as well. I've talked with many men who have taken up this spiritual discipline with real fervor.

Be creative! I know guys who use notebooks, others who use their computers, some who record their thoughts on cassette tapes, and still others who scribble thoughts all through the day on index cards or a pocket notepad. Some guys use their journals as a way to write letters to God.

Do what works for you. And if you miss a day or two, don't give up. There's no rule that you must use your journal every day, nor is there only one way to journal.

When I die, my journals and notes will be passed on to my children. There will be much encouragement for them as they see the history of my faith. They'll discover the times I wrestled with God, as well as the times I was on the mountaintop. They'll see when I wanted to "return to Egypt," as well as times where I "glowed" from being in the glory of God's presence.

I am so glad they'll be able to know me even better than they do now as a result of the journaling I've done.

Finally, let's consider one more aspect of the discipline of solitude.

A HEART FOR FASTING

Before I say anything about fasting, I freely confess my eating habits. My dietary situation is not exactly positive. Having grown up in the Philadelphia area, I love Philly cheese steaks, Tastykakes, and pizza. I believe cheesecake is a breakfast food. After all, it has the same ingredients as an omelet!

Fasting, in other words, is not something that comes naturally to me. Frankly, I don't think it comes naturally to anybody, which is partly why it can become an excellent way to reflect on God's work in our lives.

The idea behind fasting is *letting go of food*. In other words, we purposely give up meals (and snacks) in order to give our full attention to spiritual issues. Fasting is often coupled with prayer, which makes great sense. In letting go of food, we choose instead to devote an extended period of time to talking with God. And it's often in those extended sessions of prayer that God speaks to us in out-of-the-ordinary ways.

Fasting is essentially religious, but not essentially Christian. Many cults practice fasting as a means of earning favor with a god or gods. In fact, it can almost be said that fasting has become fashionable in some parts of the world. This misuse of fasting causes many Christians to be leery of the concept.

Actually, I don't remember hearing a sermon on fasting while growing up in the church. (The pastor may have preached on it, but I never "heard" it.) From my training in Bible college, seminary, and graduate school, I can't recall a single significant, positive remark or instruction dealing with fasting. Usually, if a comment was offered by a professor, it was in the negative, referring to the errors of many groups in seeking to earn eternal life through fasting or "the mortification of the flesh."

Consequently, in almost twenty years of ministry, it wasn't until the last few years that I began to hear more from Christian circles concerning fasting and became motivated to study this spiritual discipline for myself. After all, if this is something God wants me to do, I want to get in on it. At the same time, I didn't want to get caught up in the latest Christian fad or do something just because others were.

In my reading, I found many explanations of fasting that were overly detailed and extremely complex. My questions were simple: What is fasting? Why should I fast? How do I do it?

Then something happened that I'm sure was the Lord working in my life. As I was studying and praying about fasting, a crisis hit my family. *What do I do?* I thought. *Where do I turn?*

"God," I prayed, "are You there?"

That's when it struck me—not a bolt of lightning or a vision, but more like a settled sense in my mind and spirit: I was to begin a fast.

But for how long? No answer. Did this mean I had to give up pizza on Saturday night? What about buffalo wings and my beloved Philly cheese steaks?

Through all this, I began to understand how hooked I was on food. After a little more time alone, I announced to my wife and children that I was going to begin a fast. I didn't know how long it would last, but I needed them to help me by keeping food away from me.

I fasted and prayed, prayed and fasted. The days went by without much physical difficulty. I was enjoying my time with the Lord and began to think about extending my fast. Some of my friends had gone on forty-day fasts, which I greatly admired. I thought about joining them.

But on the seventh day of my fast, during my prayer time, it became clear to me that the fast was over. I think it was God's way of keeping me from spiritual pride. Through it all, I learned a valuable lesson: Fasting must begin and remain unto the Lord or it becomes of no value.

Before I go any deeper into this topic, a warning is in order: It's essential that you check with your physician before beginning a fast. Seek his or her counsel before participating to be certain it does not present a medical danger to you.

A classic book on fasting is *Fasting: A Neglected Discipline,* by David R. Smith. In it he wrote, "To the Christian, fasting is not a ritual to be indulged in regularly, but a source of intimate delight, even though it may involve heart searching and sorrow; for the value of this discipline lies not in its immediate effect but in the results which flow from its practice, and in the gradual effect which it has upon the individual believer."[2]

The design of fasting

Many things in this world serve as distractions and thus hinder our relationship with God. It would be wise to identify them and begin to seek their removal from our lives. They're what the writer of the book of Hebrews called "weights." Most of us may not consider food to be such a weight, but perhaps it's keeping us from all God wants to do. So let's examine three basic types of fasting found in the Scriptures.

Normal fast. In Luke 4:2, we read of Jesus' fast when He was in the wilderness. It states that He ate nothing during those days and was then hungry. It doesn't appear that He abstained from water, because there's no reference to His being thirsty or to a temptation set forth in that direction.

Absolute fast. In Acts 9:9, Saul (later Paul) abstained from both eating and drinking. This seems to have gone on for just a few days. Ezra 10:6 tells of Ezra going on this sort of fast. Esther and Mordecai did the same in Esther 4:16. It appears that this type of fast was followed in the midst of exceptionally difficult circumstances that called for extreme measures.

Partial fast. Daniel and his friends embarked on this type of restricted diet, we're told in Daniel 1:8–16. They voluntarily restricted their diet so as not to eat anything that would violate their conscience and divine guidelines.

The partial fast has its value. It may be the omitting of certain foods from your regular diet. Or, as a number of men around the country are now doing, it may involve the voluntary skipping of a meal or fasting until a certain time one day a week (with care not to "load up" during the other meals).

When Coach Bill McCartney first discussed his vision to reach men for Christ, he invited a group of pastors and laymen from all across Colorado to meet with him. He had set a goal of one thousand men for that first meeting. When the numbers were in, it was far short of a thousand; it was seventy-two.

But those seventy-two men committed to fast and pray for other men. They arbitrarily chose Wednesday as the day they would fast until the dinner hour. Their partial fast became the impetus to the launching of this powerful ministry that has now gone around the world.

The key biblical text concerning fasting was spoken by Jesus in the Gospel of Matthew. He said:

> *Whenever you fast, do not put on a gloomy face as the hypocrites do, for they neglect their appearance so that they will be noticed by men when they are fasting. Truly I say to you, they have their reward in full. But you, when you fast, anoint your head and wash your face so that your fasting will not be noticed by men, but by your Father who is in secret; and your Father who sees what is done in secret will reward you.* (Matthew 6:16–18 NASB)

The Lord Jesus had much to say about fasting, not only what it should look like, but also the dangers that accompany it.

Dangers in fasting

It's part of human nature to want to take something good and distort it for personal gain. Such is the case with fasting. The primary way it gets distorted is that people use it to "prove" their spiritual superiority over others. This is exactly what Jesus condemned in the Matthew passage—fasting as a prideful, arrogant display of religion.

The Jewish period of fasting took place during the busiest days in the marketplace, and that's when the proud would go on their public fasts. It would be like fasting at a mall the day after Thanksgiving; you could be sure of a magnificent crowd to watch you in your "humble" devotion to God.

To be certain they were noticed, the hypocrites Jesus vilified wouldn't bathe or otherwise take care of their appearance during their fasts. But Jesus made it clear that there's no value, other than temporary adulation, in that sort of fasting. So be careful to consider your own motives in fasting. And then be careful of how you appear to other people. Fasting is not the tiebreaker for some spiritual contest.

Delights of fasting

Rather than a temporal, momentary reward of self-gratification, Jesus offers an eternal reward that comes straight from our heavenly Father. Read Matthew 6:16–18 again. Notice that right after those words on fasting are words concerning storing up treasures in heaven.

When we purchase big-ticket items in our society, we've become accustomed to the option of an "extended warranty." Sales people motivate us by assuring us that whatever goes wrong will be covered by this extended warranty. But listen to what that implies: That oven, that car, that house—no matter what it is—needs a warranty because it won't last forever. Sure, if we take good care of our stuff, it will last a long time, but not forever.

My point? God doesn't need to offer an extended warranty! His rewards are eternal. What we reap from our private, personal fasting will be waiting for us in heaven for all eternity.

William Barclay, in his commentary on the Gospel of Matthew, listed five values of fasting that are worth repeating:

1. The value of self-discipline
2. The release from slavery to a habit
3. The preservation of the ability to do without things
4. The positive value for health
5. The enhancement of our appreciation of things[3]

Paul Anderson, a pastor in Los Angeles, suggested seven benefits to fasting in an article that appeared in *Christian Herald:*

1. Fasting intensifies my prayer efforts.
2. Fasting helps me to receive guidance.
3. Fasting helps to deliver the captives of oppression and demon possession.

4. Fasting helps to avert judgment.

5. Fasting causes me to seek help.

6. Fasting is a way to express grief.

7. Fasting is a way to pursue holiness.[4]

Anderson then quoted Andrew Murray as saying, "Fasting helps to express, to deepen, and to confirm the resolution that we are ready to sacrifice anything, to sacrifice ourselves to attain what we seek for the kingdom of God."

One of the best-known preachers from the past is Jonathan Edwards. His sermon "Sinners in the Hands of an Angry God" moved hundreds of New Englanders to repentance and faith in the early days of colonial America. In fact, that one sermon helped spark a revival known as "The Great Awakening." He was not known for a commanding voice or pulpit manner, but God used him in a mighty way nonetheless.

From a human standpoint, it's difficult to account for such far-reaching results from a single sermon. The speaker was not dynamic, nor did he use many gestures. Yet he spoke with deep sincerity.

Few knew the intense spiritual preparation Jonathan Edwards put himself through in advance of that sermon. For three days preceding the address, he did not eat a single meal—no food for seventy-two hours! On top of that, he didn't sleep for the three nights before the sermon. In place of food and rest, Edwards was on his knees, praying, "Lord, give me New England! Give me New England!"

When he rose from his knees and made his way to his pulpit on that particular Sunday, it's reported that he looked as if he had been gazing straight into the face of God. Even before he began speaking, strong conviction of their sins fell upon all those who attended the meeting.

That's the sort of encouragement I like to read about. If we commit to solitude, to journaling, and to fasting, who knows what incredible things can happen in the kingdom of God?

CHAPTER SEVEN

A HEART FOR GIVING

I need to get something off my chest. I'm tired of hearing that all the church wants is my money, or that Christians shouldn't talk about money because it will scare people away. While some churches and ministries have made the headlines in recent years because they lacked financial integrity, the truth is that they represent a tiny fraction of churches, ministries, and clergy in this country. The enemy has done a marvelous job of focusing the world's attention (and even the church's) on the handful and thereby making us paranoid or apologetic about speaking on the subject of giving.

Thus, there's a lack of teaching on giving from the pulpit, leaving many Christians struggling under the burden of runaway credit-card spending. So, although our Lord owns "the cattle on a thousand hills" (Psalm 50:10), we've got our money locked up at 10 percent interest, and numerous churches are struggling to get by.

It's common knowledge that giving to the Lord's work is not what it should be. On a proportionate basis, giving today is less than it was during the Great Depression! Even when it comes to giving to missions, on a per capita basis, we rank sixteenth, with Ireland sending out more missionaries than the American church.

We need to come to grips with what the Bible says about money. After all, Jesus spoke more about a person's possessions than He did about heaven and hell combined. You can't read far in the Bible without coming to the realization that over and over, the Scriptures associate the way we handle our finances with our spiritual maturity.

You can't separate maturity and mammon. A man's check-book and credit card statements are good barometers of his spiritual growth. I don't know about you, but that makes me uncomfortable! I'd much rather put the areas of my life into compartments and choose the ones to which God can have access. It's far easier to assume I'm doing well spiritually when I don't have to enter every compartment regularly. But, unfortunately, God doesn't operate that way. He's not interested in one or two or even three areas of Glenn's life; He wants all of me—all that I am, including the way I use my possessions—to be conformed to His image.

Many things in this world are amoral. A two-by-four piece of lumber is amoral—until I pick it up and whack you over the head with it. Then the board becomes a moral issue. It's the same way with finances. Money is amoral, but I can *love* money, making it a moral issue.

John Gardner wrote the following truths about giving:

A peculiar spiritual quality is involved in true giving. The distinctive quality has to do with the basic assumption that love must be the soil out of which all spiritually significant benevolence springs. Implied also is the contention that love for one's fellow man and love for God are inseparably one. . . . The offering of a gift requires that the donor achieve complete separation between himself and that which he gives. . . . It is important that the gift be enabled to accomplish its full work unencumbered by the personal bearing of the donor. . . . The real motive behind such gifts must be love. This love is two-dimensional. It

is both towards God and towards man. In both respects it repre-
sents the offering of self and the desire to be helpful.[1]

So what are the biblical principles that should guide our financial lives?

THE MEANS

God's Word teaches *stewardship,* which means managing things for someone else—the owner. Literally it means "the law of the house." When the master who owns the house is gone, he puts his possessions in the hands of a steward, and there are laws that govern the exercise of that steward's role.

Communism teaches that the government owns everything. Capitalism teaches that the individual owns everything. Biblical Christianity teaches that God owns everything (check out Psalm 50).

In particular, the Bible teaches us four truths about stewardship that should affect the way we manage our money. As a steward, we must remember the following?

God owns it

This is the easiest doctrine in the world to believe and the most difficult to apply. We read it throughout the Scriptures, yet most of us don't make the connection to our "stuff."

Do you believe that your house, your clothes, your car, your golf clubs, and your CD player all belong to God?

Paul described this concept in detail to the Corinthian church. They were dealing with division in their church, so the apostle used it as an illustration of proper stewardship:

Now these things, brethren, I have figuratively applied to myself and Apollos for your sakes, so that in us you may learn not to exceed what is written, so that no one of you will become arrogant in behalf of one against the other. For who regards you as superior? What do you have that you did not receive? And if you did receive it, why do you boast as if you had not received it? You are already filled, you have already become rich, you have become kings without us; and indeed, I wish that you had become kings so that we also might reign with you. (1 Corinthians 4:6–8 NASB)

The principle is that if we believe that God owns what we have, then every gift, every talent, and every dollar in our bank accounts comes from Him. Even our breath is from our Lord. There's no room for pride when giving the glory to God.

Do you know people who are blessed by God financially and then say, "We had a fantastic year! We worked our tails off!" But plenty of other folks worked just as hard and yet didn't make anywhere near as much. God simply blessed one more bountifully than the other. It wasn't a question of how hard they worked.

In addition, God gave you the ability to work, and He gave you your job. Therefore, the only appropriate response is humility. To God be the glory.

God supplies it

Sometimes our needs as we see them are not the same needs that God sees in our lives. It's a stretch to take an American's needs and apply them to other cultures. Anyone who travels internationally is aware of the raging needs and economic disparity around the world. But the truth is, what we need, God will supply. It's easy to embrace that principle when we pay our bills each month. But what about those months when we fall short? Do we really believe God will supply then?

Paul taught the church at Philippi the key to this issue. It's all about learning to be content: "Be anxious for nothing, but in everything by prayer and supplication with thanksgiving let your requests be made known to God. And the peace of God, which surpasses all comprehension, will guard your hearts and your minds in Christ Jesus" (Philippians 4:6–7 NASB).

Are you content with God's provision for you today? Whether this has been a good year or not, God will meet all your needs. The Bible offers some incredible illustrations of this truth. For example, there was a widow whose grain barrel and flask of oil never ran dry (see 1 Kings 17:14–16). God met her needs, and He told us repeatedly that He will meet ours. (For many of us, our problem may be that we've come to equate *needs* with *desires*.)

The real application here is contentment. Jesus told us not to worry about tomorrow (see Matthew 6:34). In doing so, we expend a great deal of energy on things over which we have no control.

God multiplies it

Not only does God own and supply our resources, but He also multiplies them. In Second Corinthians, we have all three of these principles stated in one verse: "Now He who supplies seed to the sower and bread for food will supply and multiply your seed for sowing and increase the harvest of your righteousness" (2 Corinthians 9:10 NASB).

God owns it; we handle it according to His directions. God supplies it; in peace, we leave our needs with Him. God multiplies it; we trust Him. Be sure to notice: Did God say He will increase the harvest of our bank account or of our righteousness? He's more concerned with how we live than with what we have.

Paul went on to say, "You will be enriched in everything for all liberality, which through us is producing thanksgiving to God. For the ministry of this service is not only fully supplying the needs of the saints, but is also overflowing through many thanksgivings to God" (2 Corinthians 9:11–12 NASB). God wants us to see that what is given to Him will result in thanksgiving to Him. Whenever we give anything to God, He will always return greater than what we gave. It's only a matter of time.

For some, this is a tremendous test of faith. But that's the principle for us to apply—trust. I believe Him enough to dig down into my wallet as an exercise of my trust. What I give, He will multiply.

Do you believe it?

God rewards it

God also rewards our faithful stewardship. This principle affects us all. Jesus spoke of it in Matthew:

Do not store up for yourselves treasures on earth, where moth and rust destroy, and where thieves break in and steal. But store up for yourselves treasures in heaven, where neither moth nor rust destroys, and where thieves do not break in or steal; for where your treasure is, there your heart will be also. (Matthew 6:19–21 NASB)

Managing our resources means placing our treasures in heaven, not in amounts of money. We can't send dollars ahead to heaven, so we use our money in giving. We invest our funds in the lives of others and in the work of the Lord.

What you treasure shows where your heart is. That is one convicting sentence.

With that in mind, let's take one more look at the spiritual discipline of giving and why we should give.

THE MOTIVATION

If we can cement the following seven principles in our thinking, they will have a positive impact on our giving patterns in the future. They explain why God wants us to be characterized by a giving spirit.

A grateful heart

After telling the church at Corinth in 2 Corinthians 9 that their giving was supplying all the needs of the saints and resulting in thanksgiving to God, Paul went on to say, "Because of the proof given by this ministry, they will glorify God for your obedience to your confession of the gospel of Christ and for the liberality of your contribution to them and to all" (2 Corinthians 9:13 NASB).

Next time you're in church, remember when the offering plate is passed that it's a time of praise, worship, and glory to God. That will change the way many of us view the offering! For some reason, many Christians have negative feelings about giving to the Lord. But it can be just the opposite. Consider what this money will do to further the work of the gospel, take care of God's people, help the poor, and say thank You to the Lord.

A submissive heart

In Genesis 14, Abraham gave one-tenth of everything he had to the Lord. The Law of Moses came more than four hundred years later, so Abraham didn't give because he was required to, but because he recognized the greatness of the One who blessed him. The principle continues today: "Honor the Lord with your wealth, with the firstfruits of all your crops; then your barns will be filled to overflowing, and your vats will brim over with new wine" (Proverbs 3:9–10 NIV).

When a man honors the Lord with his giving, he demonstrates his submission to Him. That man recognizes God's sovereignty over all, for all belongs to Him.

A joyful heart

King David understood the principle of joy as it relates to giving. He explained it to the people this way:

Since I know, O my God, that You try the heart and delight in uprightness, I, in the integrity of my heart, have willingly offered all these things; so now with joy I have seen Your people, who are present here, make their offerings willingly to You. . . . So they ate and drank that day before the Lord with great gladness. (1 Chronicles 29:17, 22 NASB)

Offering money to God is not a burden but a delight. I receive great joy when I support a missionary and he sends back a letter indicating he has recently led a young man to Christ. I get excited. I'm thankful that I'm able to help. Giving is not a hassle—it's a privilege.

A supportive heart

Have you ever asked yourself why Christians support pastors and missionaries? The prime reason is that the Bible commands it. The apostle Paul addressed this in writing to the Corinthians:

Am I not free? Am I not an apostle? Have I not seen Jesus our

Lord? Are you not my work in the Lord? If to others I am not an apostle, at least I am to you; for you are the seal of my apostleship in the Lord. . . . So also the Lord directed those who proclaim the gospel to get their living from the gospel. (1 Corinthians 9:1–2, 14 NASB)

Those who proclaim the gospel should make their living from it. Interestingly, Paul made money as a tentmaker, but the truth remains that the gospel demands full-time efforts from many people. We should consider it a privilege to send off missionaries in service of the King. I want to support the work of the gospel all over the world.

A merciful heart

The Scriptures are clear that those who are financially blessed should help those less fortunate. Consider the words of the apostle John: "But whoever has the world's goods, and sees his brother in need and closes his heart against him, how does the love of God abide in him? Little children, let us not love with word or with tongue, but in deed and truth" (1 John 3:17–18 NASB).

This issue can cause a certain amount of stress in our lives, because there are so many "con artists" out to rip us off. But the Bible is clear: Help the poor. I've developed the attitude that I would rather have the right spirit and be ripped off than to never give money to anyone because I've become cynical.

A faithful heart

A wonderful description of God's provision for us appears in Paul's writings to Corinth:

Now this I say, he who sows sparingly swill also reap sparingly; and he who sows bountifully will also reap bountifully. Each one must do just as he has purposed in his heart, not grudgingly or under compulsion, for God loves a cheerful giver. And God is able to make all grace abound to you, so that always having all sufficiency in everything, you may have an abundance for every good deed. (2 Corinthians 9:6–8 NASB)

Trust God. He will take care of you.

Here's a practical tip that has helped me in my personal finances: Set aside the amount of money you give to God *before* you figure out the rest of your budget. That way, you've made your giving to God your top priority, as well as setting up a more realistic budget.

Here's how it works: If I make $100 a week, I give the first $10 to God, and then I figure out my budget based on $90. It sounds simple, but it's a way to keep from squeezing God out of the picture.

If you're like me, you may find it's difficult to live on that hypothetical $90 a week. But if I give to God first, it puts me in the marvelous position of trusting Him to meet my needs. I need that stretching of my faith. He has never failed in the past, and I don't think He'll start failing now!

A rewarded heart

> *Instruct those who are rich in this present world not to be conceited or to fix their hope on the uncertainty of riches, but on God, who richly supplies us with all things to enjoy. Instruct them to do good, to be rich in good works, to be generous and ready to share, storing up for themselves the treasure of a good foundation for the future, so that they may take hold of that which is life indeed.* (1 Timothy 6:17–19 NASB)

I know people who think that giving to receive a heavenly reward is a carnal motivation. We use mixed messages when discussing "incentives" for service. For example, we feel it's wrong to give children candy for memorizing a Bible verse, so instead we give them a New Testament! It's still an incentive no matter how you slice it.

The Lord uses incentives and rewards in the Bible. Certainly He doesn't consider it a carnal motivation. In Matthew 19, Jesus told the rich, young ruler to sell all he had and give it to the poor so he would have treasure in heaven. Sounds like working for a heavenly reward to me.

I try to give out of love for the Lord, but the fact still remains that there's a reward on top of all that. Paul's words are strong. Don't trust in your own stuff, but trust in God and His provision for you. To do so will place you in a better position both here and in heaven.

THE METHOD

I can remember the scene like it was yesterday. My parents gathered their three boys around the kitchen table, a favorite place in our home. All of us were in our usual seats, but Mom wasn't her usual busy self. My dad tends to look stern, coming from his staid German heritage. You could always identify his mood by the corners of his eyes and mouth—the telltale Wagner smirk.

But on this occasion, he had an unusually serious look. Taking a deep breath, he unfolded to his sons the severity of the situation. We were in trouble financially.

Dad was and still is one of the hardest-working men I know. Extra work at a side job was the norm as he tried to provide for his family. He never made a lot of money, but we all respected his work ethic, simplicity of life, and the way he and Mom could stretch a dollar further than anyone.

This time, however, Dad explained that things were especially tough. "We might have to sell the house," he said.

Then he said something that I thought was completely off the wall: "Your mom and I have started tithing." Even though an accountant friend had reviewed their finances and warned against it, they wanted to trust God with everything.

Dad's tithing system was simple. He set aside an old cigar box for his tithing money. When he received his paycheck, he cashed it and placed 10 percent right off the top in that box until Sunday. No matter how late he worked on Saturday night, he never forgot to take the money from the box each Sunday morning.

In response to my parents' faith, God provided. He didn't shower them with mountains of cash, but instead of there being more month than money, there was just enough money for the month.

We never lost the house, and we boys learned a valuable lesson. My folks based their lives on biblical principles of stewardship. Though they never gave less than 10 percent, they never locked themselves into a percentage, and they never set a limit. They've continued to increase the percentage they give each year. They have no pension to speak of, and when others have retired to sit and rock, they continued to work in order to give to the Lord. They pay their own way to the mission field each year for short-term projects, and they'll do that as long as they're physically able.

Do you ever find yourself asking, "How much should I give?" That question raises the important issue that I call the principle of sacrifice, which my parents demonstrate. *Sacrifice* is almost a foreign word in our Western culture, where we're well-off compared to the rest of the world. Yet, God's Word teaches us some valuable lessons on this subject. There are at least three answers to the question of how much we should give:

1. Give generously

As we saw earlier, Paul wrote these incisive words to the believers living in Corinth: "Now this I say, he who sows sparingly will also reap sparingly; and he who sows bountifully will also reap bountifully" (2 Corinthians 9:6 NASB).

How much should we give? Give bountifully! Why?

Because we reap what we sow. We will receive what we deserve because of how we've given to the Lord. What we do affects how we're blessed both now and in the future. Don't hold back or argue with God, for He has our best interests at heart. Paul repeated the principle in Galatians, referring to the spiritual life. It works in every aspect of life.

Because God is glorified. We tend to think of glorifying God by singing, teaching, or praying. We rarely think of giving as a way for God to receive our honor, though it is as much as the other ways. The Jewish thank offering is an example of this principle at work. Paul referred to it in the passage we've already seen in 2 Corinthians 9.

I find it fascinating that when a people give themselves to

God both in time and in material things, He is glorified. We should give bountifully to insure that the praise and honor go directly to Him.

2. Give proportionately

One of the most mentioned biblical principles of giving is recorded in 1 Corinthians 16:1–2: "Now concerning the collection for the saints, as I directed the churches of Galatia, so do you also. On the first day of every week each one of you is to put aside and save, *as he may prosper,* that no collections be made when I come" (NASB, italics added).

This is called proportionate giving—giving as we have been blessed. Paul was collecting money for Jewish believers who were suffering in Judea because of famine and being ostracized from Jewish society.

I've heard so many messages on the tithe; was it really three tithes the Jews were required to pay, with the third one coming every three years, which would mean giving 23–1/3 percent per year? I've preached messages along those lines. But I've come to see that by working on a formula, I've often missed the motivation behind giving. I try to judge my spiritual maturity by the numbers, but God judges by the intent of the heart.

We read in Deuteronomy, "Now behold, I have brought the first of the produce of the ground which You, O Lord have given me. And you shall set it down before the Lord your God, and worship before the Lord your God" (Deuteronomy 26:10 NASB).

Giving proportionately, from the first of our resources, is an act of worship. My dad taught me that giving 10 percent is a great place to *start.* If that figure gets you into the habit of giving, it's a good thing. But if that's where you stop, you haven't fully understood all that both the Old and New Testaments have to say about giving.

3. Give sacrificially

Read the account of the widow and her two small coins in Luke 21:1–4. The Lord Jesus said she gave more than all the rich folks who gave out of their abundance. They gave their tithes, as the Law demanded, but she gave more than them because she gave all she had. It becomes a question not of how much we give, but of how much is left after we give. This is true sacrificial giving. Why give this way?

Because heart is more important than head. This is the key lesson from the Luke passage. The head wants to calculate a percentage and then congratulate itself for following the rules. But the heart wants to respond to God's goodness and break man's rules. The sacrifice the widow made was what set her apart from all those around her. She received God's "Well done" even though she wasn't nearly as rich as they were.

Because Jesus is our model. Paul wrote, "For you know the grace of our Lord Jesus Christ, that though He was rich, yet for your sake He became poor, so that you through His poverty might become rich" (2 Corinthians 8:9 NASB).

Christ is our example, giving Himself completely for us. That's what sacrifice is all about.

I went on a mission trip to India a number of years ago and was privileged to meet many wonderful Indian pastors and evangelists. I preached in several of the major cities, plus we traveled to some remote areas.

In one town, I was taken with the enthusiasm of the pastor and his growing congregation. They had erected a building, and without any money from the West, they were sending out their own missionaries all across the country. The pastor told me about "the joys of giving sacrificially." If ever there was a church as poor as the one in Macedonia, this was it! Yet they gave.

The pastor pointed to one small, older woman who had no sandals. "She has to walk miles to get to church," he informed me. He went on to tell me that when they had taken an offering to send workers into the spiritual harvest field, this woman removed her sandals and placed them in the plate as it was passed.

I walked over to her to speak to her through an interpreter. I commended her on her sacrifice. At first, she looked at me with a puzzled expression. Then she smiled, touched my face the way my grandma used to, and spoke to me, also through an interpreter.

"You misunderstand," she told me. "I am just happy and blessed that I had something to give."

That's giving the way Jesus intended.

CHAPTER EIGHT

A HEART FOR COMMUNICATING YOUR FAITH

I love my wife.

Those are more than just words to me. Susan and I have a special relationship. I thank God every day that He brought her into my life. The miracle of all time is that she knows me as well as she does and yet she loves me, too! I hope I never get over it.

Because I love my wife, I have a natural tendency to talk about her. When someone is as amazing as she is, I find I can't help but rave about her to almost everyone I meet. It's not a forced, contrived, or rehearsed kind of speech, either. I just speak from my heart.

I've always been intimidated, however, when I've heard other pastors and evangelists talk about how they got on a plane, asked God to open a door for presenting the gospel to the person sitting next to them, and, by the end of the flight, had led the person to Christ! Myself, I tend to pray that the person next to me will leave me alone. Some people like to talk; others of us like privacy. Don't get me wrong—I love people and enjoy ministering to them. It's just that I'm not exactly the outgoing type. Once the ice is broken, however, I do just fine.

On a recent flight, a sweet, elderly lady sat down next to me. I helped her place her oversized, overweight luggage into the overhead compartment, and then as I sat down, she started right in talking.

"Where are you from?" she asked.

I answered politely, but that was just the first of a barrage of questions:

"Are you married?"

"Do you two have children?"

Before long we were off and running, and the conversation was no longer awkward. I was eventually able to discuss the gospel with her and encourage her to trust in Christ.

The longer I've been a Christian, the more I've become convinced that communicating my faith is like discussing Susan. Just as I love her and can't help but talk about her, so it should be with presenting Christ. I love Him, and therefore I want to tell everyone what He's done for me.

Notice that my desire to talk about my love for Susan didn't result from taking a course titled "How to Tell Others About Your Love for Your Wife." No, it's a natural outflow of our love relationship. Likewise, I don't have to take a class on evangelism in order to communicate what naturally flows from my heart. While I encourage such classes and have even taught them, I prefer to let it be a natural, normal part of my life. In my mind, that's one of the biggest misconceptions in our Christian culture today. Let me state the truth in unmistakable terms:

A personal relationship with Christ will make me a powerful witness for Christ.

Therefore, the key issue in talking about my faith is to work on a growing, dynamic relationship with Christ. If that growth is happening, I won't be able to keep from talking about it.

Perhaps some clarification of terms is in order. Exactly what do we mean when we use the word *evangelism?* It can mean lots of different things to lots of different people. For me, Donald

Whitney's definition is helpful:

> *If we want to define it thoroughly, we could say that evangelism is to present Jesus Christ in the power of the Holy Spirit to sinful people in order that they may come to put their trust in God through Him, to receive Him as their Savior, and serve Him as their King in the fellowship of His Church.*[1]

So how do we do it? What are the most effective methods for reaching the lost world for Christ? How do we allow our love for Christ to pour out and affect those around us? There's been much debate in the church over methods of evangelism. But if our witness springs from our heart, the methodology isn't really such a major issue, is it? Yet, it's important to discuss different approaches to presenting Christ to the lost world. Let's examine a couple of the most popular.

COMMUNICATING YOUR FAITH: A LIFESTYLE

Witnessing starts with the way we live. There's absolutely no way to effectively explain the gospel if our lifestyle does not back up what we're saying. To use another term, we must have *integrity.*

Integrity demands that we live by the principles and guidelines set forth in God's Word. We need to be true followers of Christ if others are to see Christ within us.

Remember the apostle Peter's words: "But sanctify Christ as Lord in your hearts, always being ready to make a defense to everyone who asks you to give an account for the hope that is in you, yet with gentleness and reverence" (1 Peter 3:15 NASB).

The Christians in Peter's day were being persecuted simply for being Christians. With the fear of torture hanging over them, it's easy to imagine that many believers "went private" with their faith. No one would notice anything different about them, so they weren't bothered by the persecutors. But others lived in a way that demonstrated "hope." These people aroused such curiosity that the non-Christians were constrained to ask them,

"Why do you act the way you do? You're different. I want to know what makes you the way you are."

That's lifestyle evangelism—people seeing a life of integrity.

In his excellent book *Gentle Persuasion*, Joe Aldrich put together a list of six observations relating to lifestyle evangelism:

1. No one will receive Christ through you unless he receives you first. Love others until they want to discuss the reasons.

2. God's communicative strategy has always been to wrap an idea in a person.

3. Invest your time in individuals who seem open to faith. Look for things like their interest in your Christian company, becoming aware of the gospel's answers to their needs, curiosity, and questions. These are all positive signs to encourage your seed planting. Also, their background ceases to be a hindrance, and they take the initiative to include you in their social life.

4. The goal of lifestyle evangelism is to become part of your friends' world. Recognize their uniqueness and interests.

5. Share the gift of your need—that is, tell the story of your own spiritual need and how Christ became your Savior.

6. If you love what somebody else loves, you'll be loved.

About the same time I read Joe Aldrich, I came across an article in *Discipleship Journal* by Stephen Sorenson entitled "One Hundred Percent Natural." In it, he pointed out that when Jesus interacted with people, He didn't use evangelistic formulas but rather reached out to them. He was willing to touch lepers when other people wouldn't even stand next to them. He met folks on their own turf, asked questions, and listened as they answered. Yet many Christians today don't have any non-Christian friends. If we're going to reach people of this generation, it will only be on their turf. They won't come to us!

Sorenson went on to say that we should prepare ourselves to

discuss our faith, but nothing can replace personal interaction in the lives of others. The Lord can work through such relationships. In this process, our own relationship with Christ must be kept fresh. Otherwise we can end up offering sterile concepts about God rather than dynamic stories of what He's doing right now.

Many nonbelievers are afraid of or put off by traditional approaches to evangelism, but at the same time they're hungry for Christian individuals to love them sincerely. That means listening without judging and treating them as regular people, not as potential converts. Only in this way, Sorenson concluded, can we earn the right to speak.

We often underestimate the power of a life well lived. But let's be careful with this issue. We must not allow the concept of "letting my life speak" to become an excuse for not telling other people about Christ. Notice the progression in 1 Peter 3:15. If we truly live for Christ, it should prompt others to ask about it. Then we should be willing and ready to respond. Let's look next at how to do that.

COMMUNICATING YOUR FAITH: VERBAL WITNESSING

Witnessing may simply mean stating that you're a believer in Jesus. Many of us have a preconceived notion of verbal witnessing as fairly confrontational. But that isn't necessarily so.

As a student in Bible college, I would go with classmates from person to person on the beach in Florida or from door to door of homes, seeking to tell people about the Lord. It was a mixed bag. Sometimes I would meet a person who genuinely wanted to discuss salvation. But often I felt I was intruding on someone's personal time on the beach or at home.

I was always much more comfortable getting to know someone at work and eventually seeing the opportunity to tell him about Christ. While I greatly appreciate the lessons I learned in college, I've come to realize that different personality types and different gifts work themselves out differently. The important thing is that in some clear way, people see and hear about Jesus from me.

I've also learned how important it is to be open to every opportunity. There's no telling what would be missed if I neglected to discuss the gospel with someone. Mr. Kimball knows what I mean.

Mr. Kimball lived more than a hundred years ago. In 1858, while teaching a Sunday school class, he led to Christ a shoe clerk in Boston.

That shoe clerk, named Dwight Moody, became an evangelist and the founder of a Bible school that continues to this day. In 1879, while preaching in England, Moody awakened the evangelistic zeal in the heart of a pastor of a small church.

That pastor, Frederick B. Meyer, came to an American college campus and led to Christ a student.

That student, Wilbur Chapman, began working in area YMCAs, and through his outreach in those associations, he hired a former baseball player to do further evangelistic work for him.

That baseball player, named Billy Sunday, led thousands to Christ himself. One time, he held a crusade in Charlotte, North Carolina, where some men got so excited about evangelism that they decided to invite another evangelist to follow Sunday's Charlotte campaign.

That next evangelist, named Mordecai Hamm, held a series of meetings in which a boy trusted Jesus as his Savior.

That boy, named Billy Graham, has led tens of thousands of people to Christ.

Only eternity will reveal the tremendous impact that one Sunday school teacher, Mr. Kimball, had on the lives of others.

What do we need to cover with someone to adequately explain the plan of salvation? You can find plenty of good resources, from small pamphlets to large books, all explaining how to become a Christian. Take some time to review what's available, as you may discover something perfect for the person you're trying to reach.

For me, when I explain the gospel, I want the person to understand five points.

First, because we're all born in sin, we're all imperfect. That doesn't mean we're not "good" people by society's standards. It means we've all missed God's mark of perfection. And that imperfection makes us unable to save ourselves. I usually have a person look at a Bible verse like Isaiah 64:6 to back up this point: "For all of us have become like one who is unclean, and all our righteous deeds are like a filthy garment; and all of us wither like a leaf, and our iniquities, like the wind, take us away" (NASB).

Second, our works are incapable of making a difference. We cannot earn perfection by what we do; the Bible says clearly: "For by grace you have been saved through faith; and that not of yourselves, it is the gift of God; not as a result of works, that no one may boast" (Ephesians 2:8–9 NASB).

When you've put in a hard week at work and you receive that paycheck, you feel a sense of accomplishment. You know you've earned every cent. You may believe you're worth more than you're paid, but you've performed certain tasks and have been rewarded for doing them.

Unfortunately, people often bring this mind-set into the arena of spiritual things. That's why it's essential to understand that, from God's perspective, we cannot earn perfection.

Third, Jesus Christ made the complete payment for our sin when He died on the cross. What we could never do for ourselves, let alone for anyone else, He did for us. Two excellent texts are 2 Corinthians 5:21 ("He made Him who knew no sin to be sin on our behalf, that we might become the righteousness of God in Him" [NASB]) and 1 Peter 3:18.

I've noticed that people, particularly in our Western culture, have a difficult time receiving a gift. They may appreciate it when you offer to pick up the tab at a lunch or dinner, but there's often a look of embarrassment on their faces. Why? Because we've been taught from early on that we should provide for ourselves. "Take care of yourself!" our parents told us. "Stand on your own two feet! Don't owe anyone anything."

That's why it's difficult for a person, a man in particular, to understand that the bill for his sin has been paid. Christ paid the check and included the tip. Nothing needs to be added. Nothing *can* be added.

Fourth, by placing his complete trust in Jesus as his personal Savior, a person will be saved. A familiar verse like John 3:16 ("For God so loved the world, that He gave His only begotten Son, that whoever believes in Him shall not perish, but have eternal life"[NASB]) or Acts 16:31 makes this clear.

To trust someone means to rely on him. We trust in Jesus to save us because we can't save ourselves.

When I was a young boy, I helped my dad paint the house. The ladder didn't quite reach the peak, so Dad had me follow him as we climbed and walked up the roof. It was fun to feel as if I were standing on top of the world! Then Dad straddled the roof, gave me a paint brush, and, with his hand firmly attached to my belt, lowered me head first over the edge to paint the unreachable peak!

The thing I remember most about those few seconds of life on the edge (besides Mom's questioning comments to my father) is that I felt no fear. Why? Because I trusted my dad completely. I knew he wouldn't drop me. I was certain and secure.

It's the same way with God, our heavenly Father. Our trust is in Him. Even when we feel we're on the edge, He will never drop us.

Finally, when a person trusts Jesus as Savior, eternal life is guaranteed. Salvation is based not on our personal performance but on His perfect promises. First John 5:13 ("These things I have written to you who believe in the name of the Son of God, so that you may know that you have eternal life" [NASB]) and John 6:47 establish this fact.

There's nothing magical about these five points, but they do present the gospel simply and clearly.

I've met so many guys who feel guilty about evangelism because they feel unqualified. Frank is a great example. "I can't witness to other people because I haven't been to Bible college or seminary," he lamented one day over lunch.

"Do you really believe you have to have that level of training to share your faith?" I quizzed.

"Well, that might be a bit of an overstatement," he conceded. "But I'll be honest, Glenn, evangelism scares me."

"Why?" I asked.

"Because I just know I'll start talking to someone, and he'll ask me questions about heavy theological issues about which I'm clueless. I figure it's better for me to just leave the whole thing alone and trust the professionals to handle it rather than begin a project I can't finish. I guess I have no business sharing my faith."

His answer didn't surprise me. But I persisted: "Why do you think this way?"

"Well, a friend of mine got into this giant theological debate with a coworker," he answered. "They started talking about issues like creation versus evolution, why God would allow suffering and evil in the world, what about all the other religions in the world, and a bunch of other issues that made my head spin just hearing about them. I would've had no idea how to answer any of those questions."

So many of us can be frightened away from witnessing by other people's experiences. The more Frank and I talked, the more I was able to convince him that not everyone has to achieve "Super Debater/Defender of the Faith" status in God's kingdom. On the other hand, I did encourage him to invest in a few books and tapes that provide basic answers to the more common questions people ask. Ignorance is a poor excuse.

If Frank's argument sounds like one you've used, I would offer you the same encouragement. You really can communicate your faith verbally to other people. It's not as difficult or as tricky as you might think. Leave the guilt behind you, and begin praying about this issue. Ask the Lord to lead you to just the right person to begin a dialogue with about your faith. After all, it's normal to talk about the One you love.

COMMUNICATING YOUR FAITH: PRACTICAL REMINDERS

Leroy Eims of The Navigators suggests five elements as "musts" if our evangelism is to be effective. I couldn't agree more, so here they are in summary form:

Stick-to-it-iveness

It may take some time to reach people for Christ. We can't

be naive and think that all will come to the Lord after hearing the gospel message just once. Many folks take years before deciding to accept Christ as their Savior. Our job is to be consistent. That's all we can do.

Friendship, not conquest

The purpose of communicating our faith is to gain a brother or sister in Christ, not to carve another notch in our evangelistic gun belts. That sounds a bit silly, but you know as well as I do that this mentality exists in some churches. Let's make a friend, not try to capture prey.

Control and guidance of the Holy Spirit

Explaining our faith in Jesus is just like every other aspect of our lives—it should be done under the influence of the Holy Spirit. It's not an activity that we conjure up the courage to pull off, just as we don't "psyche ourselves up" to talk with God in prayer. We allow the Holy Spirit to work through us. We are the vessels; He is the treasure.

Simplicity and clarity of the message

Presenting the gospel to an unbeliever is not an opportunity for a Christian to show off how much theology he knows. People want answers in a form they can understand. Don't use religious jargon that will come off as meaningless to an unchurched person. Practice explaining the plan of salvation with the simplest terms possible. Make it clear.

A life that shows forth the message

We can't talk about how wonderful the abundant life is if we make Ebenezer Scrooge look like a choirboy. It comes back to integrity. Our lives and our message must complement each other rather than contradict. People will notice the difference in our lives and may even ask about it.

When I came to Christ, I traveled for a full year with a Christian music group. It was an experience for which I'm eternally grateful. During the two weeks of music camp, where we learned the music and got to know each other (after all, we would be together for the next ten months, visiting thirty-eight states and eight foreign countries), several of the group's members led us in Bible studies and classes on evangelism.

It was an exciting time for me, learning about how to discuss my faith with others. Finally the day arrived when I had my first opportunity. Our initial tour stop was in upstate New York, where we were booked to perform at a local high school. After the concert, we were given tracts to hand out to the students in order to engage them in conversation about the Lord.

My excitement waned quickly. It just wasn't my day. I felt so defeated. I either couldn't get kids to talk to me or, when they did, they had absolutely no desire to trust in Christ. To make matters worse, even when we performed in churches in the following weeks, people were either already believers or not interested.

This went on for some time. Disappointment followed disappointment. Failures heaped up on failures. What was I going to do? Give up? Become a silent Christian? Leave it to the professionals? Let my life do the talking? Conclude that evangelism just wasn't my gift?

Then I learned one of the most important lessons of my Christian life:

I can't save anybody. My responsibility is to be faithful to love Jesus, to live for Him, and to speak of Him. God will bless my faithfulness.

Eventually, God allowed me to see people come to Christ through my witness. And I've since learned that the joy of that process never grows old. But that lesson has stayed with me over the years. I'm not into scalp hunting for Jesus to hang them on my belt and show off at church.

By the way, the music group I was in went up into Canada for a series of concerts, and I had the opportunity to once again discuss my faith with students one on one. Following one concert, I engaged a student in a conversation about the Lord.

I did it just as I had done it the many times before. As I described the plan of salvation, it was all leading to the final question, "Would you like to receive God's gift of eternal life?" I had been told no so many times before that I had learned to brace myself for the inevitable negative response.

Once again, I was ready for my graceful closing and tactful exit. But he caught me completely off guard by answering, "Yes, I would."

In my shock, I replied, "Really?"

We both laughed and then proceeded. I have never forgotten the joy and thrill of that moment when this young student prayed to receive Christ.

The words of the following poem have a way of penetrating my soul when I consider the importance of developing a heart for communicating my faith.

A Voice from Eternity

You lived next door to me for years;
We shared our dreams, our joys, our tears.
A friend to me you were indeed—
A friend who helped me when in need.
My faith in you was strong and sure;
We had such trust as should endure.
No spats between us ever rose;
Our friends were alike, also our foes.
What sadness, then, my friend, to find
That after all, you weren't so kind.
The day my life on earth did end,
I found you weren't a faithful friend.
For all those years we spent on earth,
You never talked of Second Birth,
You never spoke of my lost soul
And of the Christ who'd make me whole.
I plead today from hell's cruel fire
And tell you now my last desire:
You cannot do a thing for me,

No words today my bonds will free.
But do not err, my friend, again,
Do all you can for souls of men.
Plead with them now quite earnestly
Lest they be cast in hell with me.
                                    Author Unknown

CHAPTER NINE

FINISHING WELL

Have you ever lived in a house best described as a fixer-upper? I have. As a matter of fact, I still do. My wife kiddingly tells me that God loves me, but *she* has a wonderful plan for the rest of my life—fixing up our house so that it's presentable.

Fortunately, she's patient. We have so many half-completed projects around our house that it's embarrassing. I've learned over the years that it's not enough to make a decision to do something; I actually have to get in there and do it.

WHAT IT TAKES TO FINISH WELL

What does it take to complete projects—including the development of the spiritual disciplines in our lives—and do a good job in the process? I can think of seven important factors, as well as the Scriptures that affirm their necessity:

Time

For any project to be completed well, we must set aside the time to do the job right. My home-improvement rule of thumb is that a job usually takes twice as long as I planned.

Consider the wise writer of the Old Testament book of Ecclesiastes:

There is an appointed time for everything. And there is a time for every event under heaven—

A time to give birth and a time to die;

A time to plant and a time to uproot what is planted.

A time to kill and a time to heal;

A time to tear down and a time to build up.

A time to weep and a time to laugh;

A time to mourn and a time to dance.

A time to throw stones and a time to gather stones;

A time to embrace and a time to shun embracing.

A time to search and a time to give up as lost;

A time to keep and a time to throw away.

A time to tear apart and a time to sew together;

A time to be silent and a time to speak.

A time to love and a time to hate;

A time for war and a time for peace. (Ecclesiastes 3:1–8 NASB)

How are you using your time? Are you as structured and diligent as this passage advocates? If not, don't be discouraged—neither am I! But I do use this as a goal to press toward. I want to use my time wisely.

Energy

Even if I have the time to finish something, if I'm mentally or physically exhausted, I'm not going to be productive. So I need energy to complete the task. As Christians, we have an exceptional source of power, the Holy Spirit.

But you will receive power when the Holy Spirit has come upon you; and you shall be My witnesses both in Jerusalem, and in all Judea and Samaria, and even to the remotest part of the earth. (Acts 1:8 NASB)

That He would grant you, according to the riches of His glory, to be strengthened with power through His Spirit in the inner man. (Ephesians 3:16 NASB)

Now, that's an energy source! We have available all the power we'll ever need to finish the course well.

Resources

If I'm going to paint the family room, it's vital that I have paint, brushes, rollers, pans, rags, drop cloths, and a variety of other materials to insure that the job gets done right.

Paul taught the Corinthian believers all about their resources for the Christian life:

And He has said to me, "My grace is sufficient for you, for power is perfected in weakness." Most gladly, therefore, I will rather boast about my weaknesses, that the power of Christ may dwell in me. Therefore I am well content with weaknesses, with insults, with distresses, with persecutions, with difficulties, for Christ's sake; for when I am weak, then I am strong. (2 Corinthians 12:9–10 NASB)

The apostle John taught of the same sort of resource available to believers: "You are from God, little children, and have overcome them; because greater is He who is in you than he who is in the world" (1 John 4:4 NASB).

That's a pretty impressive set of drop cloths, rollers, brushes, and paint, wouldn't you agree?

Encouragement

Many folks don't consider encouragement essential, but no one can dispute that it's so much easier to do a job when someone comes alongside you to offer praise and encouragement for what you're doing.

The apostle Paul constantly encouraged those to whom he wrote. Consider two examples, one sent to the Roman believers, the other to the church at Ephesus.

*Now may the God of hope fill you with all joy and peace in be-
lieving, so that you will abound in hope by the power of the
Holy Spirit.* (Romans 15:13 NASB)

*Now to Him who is able to do exceeding abundantly beyond all
that we ask or think, according to the power that works within
us, to Him be the glory in the church and in Christ Jesus to all
generations forever and ever. Amen.* (Ephesians 3:20–21
NASB)

Desire

I work so much more effectively when I *want* to, as opposed
to feeling forced into something. (This is probably a key reason
so much of our house is still in the fixer-upper stage.)

King David knew the value of motivation. He knew he
served God better when his heart was right.

*I delight to do Your will, O my God; Your Law is within my
heart.* (Psalm 40:8 NASB)

*Delight yourself in the Lord; and He will give you the desires of
your heart.* (Psalm 37:4 NASB)

I love that word *delight*. It brings a smile to my face just
reading it. To know that God has that sort of interest in my life
truly is a delight. Desire in the Christian life is not a difficult
thing that needs to worked up. Even a casual reading of His
Word should create a wonderful desire within us.

Ability to picture the end result

The ability to picture the end result of a project clearly sep-
arates Susan and me. She can look at it and see the potential; re-
grettably, all I see is a big mess.

Paul, like Susan, could see the possibilities:

*As a result, we are no longer to be children, tossed here and
there by waves and carried about by every wind of doctrine, by*

the trickery of men, by craftiness in deceitful scheming; but speaking the truth in love, we are to grow up in all aspects into Him who is the head, even Christ. (Ephesians 4:14–15 NASB)

I have fought the good fight, I have finished the course, I have kept the faith. (2 Timothy 4:7 NASB)

Paul was clear on his life's race. Sometimes you and I need a gentle reminder of the importance of finishing well.

While on a recent flight, I heard the captain's voice come over the loudspeaker to make the following familiar announcement: "Flight attendants, please prepare for landing."

Immediately a flight attendant followed the captain's message with her own: "Ladies and gentlemen, the captain's announcement means he has found the airport, so you must now return your seat backs to their full upright and most uncomfortable position."

We all laughed at her comment about the captain's "finding the airport." But the truth is, in order to finish well, we've got to know where we're going. Where is the "airport" at which we want to "land"?

Ability to start small and prioritize the projects

If I expect any success in big projects, I have to be able to break them down into smaller, more manageable pieces. Then I can prioritize the smaller projects in order of their importance.

Once again, consider a few words from the New Testament:

Take pains with these things; be absorbed in them, so that your progress will be evident to all. Pay close attention to yourself and to your teaching; persevere in these things, for as you do this you will ensure salvation both for yourself and for those who hear you. (1 Timothy 4:15–16 NASB)

Therefore leaving the elementary teaching about the Christ, let us press on to maturity, not laying again a foundation of repentance from dead works and of faith toward God, of instruction about washings and laying on of hands, and the resurrection of the dead and eternal judgment. (Hebrews 6:1–2 NASB)

Notice that both passages teach a process of starting at a basic point and then moving on, growing, and maturing in our faith. Starting small and prioritizing is the only effective way to accomplish any big goal. For me to fix up my house, I need to start with the easier projects, working my way up to the more difficult ones.

For many of us guys, our spiritual lives are a lot like a fixer-upper house. It's time for us to dedicate ourselves to cleaning it up. I'm asking all of us to put in the time, energy, resources, encouragement, and desire necessary to make the practice of the spiritual disciplines a daily reality. Picture how it would look if we did it!

WE'RE IN THIS PROJECT TOGETHER

Picture with me the first day of football practice in preparation for the coming season. Hopes are high. Will this be the season we make it all the way to the Super Bowl? You look around training camp at the guys who are here with you. It's obvious you've worked hard to stay in shape in the off-season, but some of your teammates don't appear to have spent much time pursuing the discipline of fasting! You begin to feel a bit proud about your conditioning when the coach blows the whistle, signifying it's time to head over to the practice field.

It's a hot and humid day, and before long the sweat begins to flow. Some guys get cramps, muscles are stretched, and bruises appear, but you make it through the day.

The coach, however, isn't happy.

Not only does he get after all those guys in poor shape, but he starts to get after you as well! "We're a team!" he yells. "We're in this together!" Then he points a finger at you, telling you to look around. "You're responsible for the others!" he screams. "You need them, and they need you!"

At first you're angry. It doesn't seem fair. Why should you be responsible for someone else? It may take you a while to fully understand the lesson, but the truth remains. We need each other. Some guys don't learn it until Super Bowl Sunday—but eventually they do learn it.

Susan and I had just flown into Charlotte, North Carolina, and were meeting with friends for a late-night snack. Somehow the conversation turned to the subject of finishing well, and Bob related the following story.

When he played football for Clemson University, the players were all required to run a predetermined distance within a certain amount of time. The time was set according to your position—lineman, back, kicker, and so on.

As some of the players struggled to get around the track within the allotted time, players who had already finished would run up alongside the other guys, yelling and cheering them on until they made it. As Bob put it, "Once you completed your race, it was expected that you would go back and find someone to encourage in order to see that he finished well."

He added, "That's the way it should happen among Christian men. We don't run this thing alone!"

A number of years ago, God told His people to get out on the field with the rest of His team and make sure they succeed. The Divine Coach wants every team member to finish well. He so desires this that He has recorded guidelines in His Word for His team.

The bottom line: You have a lot of teammates in your quest for spiritual discipline. That fact can be the stimulus we need to do something more than we've done in the past.

The New Testament has much to say about relating to one another as Christians. Consider a few examples:

We're members of one another

"So we, who are many, are one body in Christ, and individually members one of another" (Romans 12:5 NASB).

We're a team. We're in this thing together, and it will take all of us to get to the "Super Bowl."

We're devoted to one another

"Be devoted to one another in brotherly love" (Romans 12:10a NASB).

On this team, we're not to tear each other apart but build each other up. That's tough sometimes, but we don't give up on each other.

We honor one another

"Honor one another above yourselves" (Romans 12:10b NIV).

We don't dishonor one another on this team, in private or in public. We put our teammates first.

We're of the same mind

"Now may the God who gives perseverance and encouragement grant you to be of the same mind with one another according to Christ Jesus" (Romans 15:5 NASB).

We're to have no personal agendas. We have one goal, not many. That's how we will get to the "Super Bowl."

We accept one another

"Accept one another, then, just as Christ accepted you, in order to bring praise to God" (Romans 15:7 NIV).

We come from a lot of different backgrounds. We have racial differences and denominational differences, but none of that is important now because we're on God's team. We accept one another because of this new identity.

We admonish one another

"And concerning you, my brethren, I myself also am convinced that you yourselves are full of goodness, filled with all knowledge and able also to admonish one another" (Romans 15:14 NASB).

We don't flatter each other on this team. If that's what you want, go somewhere else. To flatter someone is to tell him what's not true to make him feel better about himself. I don't want that nonsense on my team. I want us to be so committed to each other that we'll tell each other the truth, the hard stuff, because we can't improve and excel without it.

We serve one another

"You, my brothers, were called to be free. But do not use your freedom to indulge the sinful nature; rather, serve one another in love" (Galatians 5:13 NIV).

We're here for each other. We're here to help you succeed.

We bear one another's burdens

"Bear one another's burdens, and thereby fulfill the law of Christ" (Galatians 6:2 NASB).

Some of us will have our share of pain and struggle this year. From marital problems to business ventures that go sour to problems with our kids, we'll run the gamut. But we'll help one another through it. We'll get the kind of help each man needs to succeed.

We submit to one another

"Submit to one another out of reverence for Christ" (Ephesians 5:21 NIV).

For the sake of the team, we put our teammates first. We don't need any spoiled brats or prima donnas around here.

We encourage one another.

"Therefore encourage one another and build each other up" (1 Thessalonians 5:11 NIV).

What happens when someone messes up by missing a blocking assignment, dropping a pass, or fumbling the ball? It's often the difference between winning teams and losing teams— winners help their teammates shake off the disappointments and get back in the game.

It's important to remind ourselves that this process takes time. Godliness doesn't happen overnight. One of my favorite comedians is Yakov Smirnoff, the Russian comic who now resides in Branson, Missouri. Several years ago, Susan and I got to attend one of his performances. I especially enjoyed the routine in which he recounted his first trip to an American grocery store.

As he walked down an aisle, he came across a jar of orange powder. The directions said to just add water and you'd have orange juice. With complete amazement, Yakov exclaimed, "What a country!"

He continued his journey down another aisle and found a white powder that, when mixed with water, gave you milk. Again he exclaimed, "What a country!"

Walking down a third aisle, he was unable to contain himself when he saw a small container labeled "Baby Powder."

"What a country!"

We do, in fact, live in an instant society. We have instant coffee, instant dinners, dial-a-date, and so on. Unfortunately, we bring the "instant" mind-set into our relationship with Christ as well, and it just doesn't work that way. This is yet one more compelling reason we need the feedback of others to keep on course and finish the race.

We really do need each other. I need you just as much as you need me. I've observed this phenomenon all over the world. When men who have a heart for God come together in a relationship, committed to being accountable to one another, they stimulate each other toward godliness.

SUCCESS FROM FAILURE

Some of us read the words of this chapter with discouraged eyes. We've tried to be committed to godliness before, but somehow we've never quite pulled it off. You may be silently saying to yourself, *What will make this time any different from the failures in my past?*

Failure is difficult, but it's not always bad. Thomas Edison, the great inventor, certainly had his share of failed experiments. He refused to allow any member of his team to use the word *failure,* however. "We have just participated in another educational experience," he would say.

Some say that failure is the back door to success. If you're like me, some days you can't even find the door. But we must come to understand that we can use failure as a means to a successful end.

For most of us, success is no more than a recovery from a string of failures, flops, and foibles. We fit right in with the folks listed in Hebrews 11. While that chapter is often called "God's Hall of Fame of Faith," to me it's really a "Hall of Reclaimed Failures."

In high school, we had a guy on the cross-country team who loved the beginning of each race but hated the finish. When the gun was fired to start the race, he would leap out in front. It wasn't long before he was way ahead of everyone else. He was usually able to maintain his lead for the first mile or so, enjoying the cheers of folks along the course.

By the time he reached the halfway point, however, he was usually sucking wind. He would watch as runners passed him, gaining a substantial lead over him. No matter what his coaches said or did, they couldn't get him to control his excitement and his desire to hear the cheers at the start. Because of this quirk, he was never able to finish a race among the leaders.

Unfortunately, many of us do the same thing in the spiritual race the Lord has called us to run. But whether we *start* well or poorly, we can still *finish* well. The Christian life is not a 100-yard dash. It's a marathon. Even though we may have stumbled at the beginning or somewhere along the way, we can get back in the race and finish strong.

CHAPTER TEN

IT'S A "WE" THING

We need each other, men. The words of God "It is not good for man to be alone" extend well beyond the marriage relationship.

One Sunday as my wife and I were walking into church, we heard a familiar song being played by the worship team. I was startled to realize why the song was familiar—it was the theme song from an old television show! And not just any TV show, but *Cheers!*

The pastor used it as a way to illustrate his theme. "The church is supposed to be a place of community, a place of family," he began. "The world has many counterfeits, many counterparts, but the church has the reality."

As he continued to develop his point, he chose the words of the theme song to drive home his point: "The church should be the place *where everybody knows your name.*"

Scripture describes the church in relational terms, such as a body, a family, and a household, as well as all the "one another" passages in the New Testament. You and I need each other. Yet many of us are more interested in pursuing programs than in pursuing relationships. I don't know anywhere in the Bible, however, where God commands the church to run better programs. He does, however, emphasize caring for one another. Whether we're considering widows or orphans or those in ministry, the clear idea is that we need each other.

I can hear someone shouting in loud protest, "That sounds like codependency to me!"

My answer is, "No, it's not!"

Codependency means I can't survive without you, which is not what we're talking about. We're talking about interdependency, meaning a community of people who need one another if they're to become all that God intends for them to be. It's the concept of mutuality. Think of it as spurring one another on to love and good works, as the writer of Hebrews exhorted. It's challenging and encouraging one another.

It's Moses with his Joshua and Jethro. It's David with his Jonathan. It's Paul and Barnabas and the group that traveled with them. It's knowing that I'm not alone in my stand. The Lord will use others in the body of Christ to help me walk with Him.

To use the words from another theme song, consider the phrase from the movie *Ghostbusters*—"Who you gonna call?"

Their answer? Ghostbusters! When things are scary and you're not sure what's happening, call them. But the truth is, when things are difficult or scary or you're facing temptation, the number to call is that of one of your brothers in Christ who can help you.

I have a database of names and phone numbers of Christian men around the world whom I've had the privilege of meeting over the last few years. They're solid, godly men in whom I place great respect. When I need input, or when I need to be challenged, encouraged, and even rebuked, I know I can call Stan, Glen, Rod, another Glen, or three or four other guys who will always be there for me. I also have men I've ministered with, guys like Dale or Rick who would never be too busy to take my call (even if it was collect). These are special guys who have created a covenant relationship with me for life. They don't always tell me what I want to hear, but they tell me what I need to hear.

One of the primary weaknesses of my life is the buying and

reading of books (with golf running a close second). I don't limit myself to religious books, either. I buy biographies, mysteries, novels, and so on. On a recent trip to my favorite supergigantic bookstore, complete with coffee bar and comfortable chairs, I wandered through the business section. I was looking for books on leadership and planning.

It was amazing to me how many books had the word *team* in their title or subtitle. Picking out a few that caught my eye, I settled into an easy chair with my decaf skinny mocha grande whipped cream latte (the decaf neutralizes the caffeine in the mocha, and the skinny neutralizes the fat in the whipped cream—at least in my mind).

These books were filled with a concept unheard of in management circles a few years ago—teamwork and relationships. In the past, everything was "from the top down." But that created an oppressive and legalistic approach to management.

Then things started to change. Leadership began to be defined in relational terms. Managers were encouraged to become involved in the lives of those they managed. The next logical step was to introduce the relational concept through the use of teams. The thinking was that through a group, we have a far greater capacity than we do as individuals. We can accomplish so much more if we work together. It maximizes effectiveness and minimizes individual weakness.

The *Harvard Business Review* published an article in its March-April 1993 issue titled "The Discipline of Teams." In it, the authors, John Katzenbach and Douglas Smith, examined this phenomenon sweeping the business community. They concluded that teamwork may, in fact, be the buzzword of the '90s, yet it must be more than just a word if it's to be effective.

The distinction between real teams and other kinds of work groups centers on performance, they said. What defines a team is the "collective work project." By that they mean a project that must be worked on together, for it cannot be produced alone.

"There is a basic discipline that makes teams work," the two researchers concluded. The most effective teams have relatively few members, a common commitment, a well-defined purpose, specific and measurable performance goals, and *individual and group accountability.*

The challenge of using teams to accomplish organizational purposes is to make sure a team has a specific purpose that makes it distinctive, requiring all its members to "roll up their sleeves and accomplish something beyond individual end-products."

These concepts have implications and applications for us as Christians who need to have a degree of accountability in our lives. A distinctive purpose sets a group apart from anything else we do. Our purpose? To grow in godliness.

The books emphasizing teamwork swept American business, because it took us a while to realize that the rugged individualism we promoted for so long just doesn't cut it.

But God knew it all along. He told us:

> *Two are better than one because they have a good return for their labor. For if either of them falls, the one will lift up his companion. But woe to the one who falls when there is not another to lift him up. Furthermore, if two lie down together they keep warm, but how can one be warm alone? And if one can overpower him who is alone, two can resist him. A cord of three strands is not quickly torn apart.* (Ecclesiastes 4:9–12 NASB)

It's all about being accountable to one another.

A HEART FOR ACCOUNTABILITY

I really believe in the meaning that lies behind the term *accountability*. The term itself, I don't care for.

Accountability can have a negative connotation. In some ways, the word sounds like the sort of highly intense feeling that would come over you when you learn you're being audited by the Internal Revenue Service. Believe me, one of my goals in life is not to link brothers up with the IRS!

I was once asked to help a man assess why every men's accountability group he ever started had failed—miserably. By the time he came to me, he was on his third or fourth group, and he was panicked that his current group was beginning to disintegrate as well. I agreed to attend the next meeting later in the week.

Upon my arrival, I observed how this guy took charge. Men were directed to take their seats, refreshments were handed out with military precision, and exactly at the appointed hour he sat down to "lead" the "meeting."

I couldn't believe what happened next.

Since I have the gift of sarcasm, it was all I could do to contain myself. He began to ask questions of these guys as if he were a district attorney on a relentless quest to uncover any secret sin in their lives! He went through his list of questions, all the while declaring himself relatively free from any impurity. After every man was thoroughly examined, he prayed a closing prayer and dismissed the men, who obediently left the room.

Once we were alone, he asked my opinion of the meeting—which I freely gave him. I had to tell him that I almost wished I was a part of his group so I could have the pleasure of quitting! I tried to explain to him the balance between accountability and affirmation. Caring and encouraging can really build trust. It's possible to be accountable in a positive context.

Yet there are others for whom accountability can sound like that teacher or coach who could never be pleased no matter how hard you worked. This man wasn't all that helpful as an instructor, either, which made the whole situation even more frustrating. Being accountable to this guy was far from a positive experience.

To someone else, on the other hand, accountability can sound like the sword your boss is dangling over your head if you don't deliver the goods. You know the kind of manager I am talking about, right? He's the sort of person who places many demands on you but only checks on your progress a day or two before the deadline. This guy is the poster child for stress, ulcers, and high blood pressure.

Wouldn't it be nice to have a different kind of boss—the sort of guy who checks in with you all along the way, not just at the end? The kind of person who believes in you? The kind who's with you through the entire process, assisting and offering needed motivation and instruction? Now, there's a more positive spin on *accountability*.

In my own dealings with Christian brothers, I have a description that works better for me than *accountability*. I like using the term *covenant relationship*. The main thing I like about it is that it highlights the fact that every person in the relationship has responsibilities. Thus, it fosters a greater feeling of mutuality. That's an important addition to any relationship.

What are the essential elements of a covenant relationship?

Trust

I trust you and you trust me. I know you have my best interests in mind and that my life and its shortcomings won't end up as a public announcement in a Wednesday evening prayer service!

Commitment

You won't leave me when I mess up. Instead, you'll follow the biblical pattern in helping me. You won't condone sin in my life, but your confrontation will be seasoned with grace, love, and forgiveness.

Honesty

You'll tell me what I need to hear, not just what I want to hear. Sometimes they'll be the same thing, but other times there will be great disparity between the two. You'll help me see the difference.

In a covenant relationship, all things are out in the open. Hard questions still need to be asked. There's still a desire to get to the heart of the matter. There's still that sense of belonging that commands respect. But the framework is more clearly defined. These guys believe in me and support me—to the point that it's OK to experience failure.

Failure within a covenant relationship leads to *restoration*.

Failure within an IRS auditing accountability group leads to *condemnation* and *isolation*.

The difference is pretty clear, don't you think?

A SPECIAL RELATIONSHIP

I once heard a football player reminisce on his years as a member of the National Football League. The record books stated that this guy was one of the oldest players before his eventual retirement. The questions he was most often asked were, "Why did you play so long? Why did you put your body through the battering, the bruising, and the injuries too numerous to mention? Why didn't you just retire earlier like so many of your counterparts?" I found his thoughtful answer intriguing:

"Why? Because I can't find anyplace else what I can get in the huddle. The fans don't experience it, the coaches don't experience it, and those on the bench don't experience it.

"But there in the huddle, your race or religion don't matter. You are a team made up of men who believe in you. If you miss a block, they run your way again because they tell you they know you can take that guy out this time. If a man fumbles the ball, they give it to him again because they believe in him. They challenge and motivate and encourage like no other place I've ever been."

That's the atmosphere that should characterize Christian groups. The church should be a place for holy huddles, where the team helps you stay on course.

Once, while ministering on the West Coast, I had the opportunity to visit with an old friend. Sammy now lives in Walnut Creek, California, a suburb of San Jose. A successful computer programmer, Sammy posed a question on the second day of our visit: "Glenn, how'd you like to accompany me to my accountability group tomorrow morning?"

"Sure," I responded.

"It's early," he razzed, knowing my disdain for anything predawn.

"How early is early?" I asked sheepishly.

"We meet at a local coffee shop at 6:00 A.M."

"OK," I replied, "but only because you're a good friend!"

The next morning, we drove a few miles down the freeway to the appointed place at the appointed hour. Sammy introduced me to the other four guys in the group. Frank, Andy, George, and Wayne were excited to have me join them.

"What's this meeting all about?" I asked, knowing the answer but wanting to hear how each of them would respond.

"This is our life-support system," George answered. "We've been together now for five years, and through that time we've been able to help each member through a crisis or two."

"Yeah, if it hadn't been for this group, I don't think I would have made it," echoed Wayne. "When my marriage came apart a couple of years ago, I was about ready to take my own life. But these guys watched over me, prayed with me, invited me over for meals, drove me to church—whatever it took to be a friend. God blessed me with these sorts of friends."

"We all have similar stories to tell," Andy added. "My marriage is strong, but I was the victim of a downsizing operation at my job. When I was out of work, I felt completely worthless as a human being. These guys refused to allow me to think that way. Their love, prayers, and support saw me through the tough times. I'm working again, thank the Lord, but I'll never forget the impact these guys had on my day-to-day life."

"These are amazing stories," I said, feeling all over again the value of accountability.

"My fifteen-year-old son got pretty messed up on drugs," Frank volunteered. "Our group had just started meeting, so we were all a little tentative about really opening up to one another."

The other guys smiled broadly, recalling those early days in the group when much of the cohesion had yet to be established.

"Anyway," Frank continued, "I decided the night before we met that I needed to tell these guys what was going on with my son. It was a risky thing to do, but I needed to hear some counsel from an objective source."

"Did you get the counsel you wanted?" I asked.

Frank smiled again. "Actually, I did get some advice, but the most important thing that came out of that meeting was just the fact that I knew I had some guys who would listen to me and not condemn me."

"That crisis was the impetus that brought us together as a group," Sammy interjected. "In those ten minutes when Frank was explaining his need, everyone else realized that we needed one another. We've been accountable to one another ever since. It's been exactly what we've needed in our lives."

"What's your format for your weekly meeting?" I inquired.

"We read a book together," Sammy replied. "Each week, we're all responsible to read the next chapter in the book and be prepared to discuss it."

"But there are lots of weeks when we never get to the book!" George added quickly.

"Why's that?" I asked.

"Because the first item on our agenda is to go around the circle and ask about every guy's life. What was this last week like? How are things at home? Your wife? Your kids? How's the job? What's going on in your personal life? These are important questions that need to be answered. Many weeks, a guy will share a difficult situation in his life that will cause us all to concentrate on how we can be of help during his time of need."

"Wow," was all I could say.

"And every meeting ends with a time of prayer for one another," George continued. "If someone is having a particularly difficult time, he's the topic of our entire prayer time. The book can wait, because we're helping a brother in need."

It was a wonderful example of accountability in action.

In an article titled "Accountability That Makes Sense" in *Leadership* journal, Gary Downing wrote passionately. Summarizing his thoughts, he suggested the following ideas as guidelines and cautions to protect the parties involved in a relationship of this nature:

1. Advice or criticism is not offered unless requested.

2. "We weren't each other's therapists but rather friends who would help the other in the spiritual life."

3. The friendship allows honesty and candor in working through struggles as major as money, sex, and power. The longevity of such a relationship heightens its worth, as each person gains a historical view of the other's life. Neither is able to con the other, and complete openness

and honesty are the result. The relationship remains a fourth priority—after God, wives, and vocation. The openness and support of the relationship carry over into other relationships and struggles.[1]

Accountability is valuable, but it involves taking a risk. The story is told of a woman who lost her life's savings in a bogus investment scheme sold to her by a skillful swindler. When her money disappeared, her dreams were shattered. In desperation, she went to the Better Business Bureau.

"Why didn't you call us first?" they asked.

The woman hung her head.

"Didn't you know about us?" the representative continued.

"Of course I did!" she replied sincerely. "I've known about your organization for years."

"So why didn't you contact us?"

Her response said it all: "I was scared to talk to you because I was afraid you would tell me no."

As Christians, we can display a similar attitude. Perhaps we start by getting involved in a course of action we already have doubts about. Or we continue in a habit that we think might be questionable. What we're doing could even be in direct violation of God's Word. But we refuse to consult with anyone because our minds are already made up. The result is sorrow and regret—all because we were afraid we would be told no.

YOU CAN DO IT

With the help of your imagination, I want you to think about what's possible when a man gets serious about the spiritual disciplines. Can you see a man whose life corresponds to his heart? Deep inside, he really wants to love and serve God. Now, through the addition of some important characteristics, he demonstrates his love for God on the outside as well:

- *He loves his Bible.* He's committed to reading it, studying it, listening to sermons, memorizing important passages, and even meditating on it. Sure, he misses a day here and there, but he's far more consistent than he has ever been in the past, and he can see the difference in his life.

- *He has learned the value of prayer in a personal way.* He can "pick up that phone" and talk to the Lord whenever he wants. He's learning the importance of praying as Jesus would pray. Discerning the will of God is clearer now that he's disciplined in his prayer life.

- *He has a new appreciation for worship.* It's more than a Sunday ritual for him. Now it's a rich, full, and vibrant part of his spiritual life. He knows the value of corporate and private worship. And it has made a significant difference in the way he relates to God.

- *He has discovered a new discipline in his life, the discipline of solitude.* With the help of this new skill, he has begun a spiritual journal to chronicle his journey with the Lord. He's even venturing into the realm of fasting in order to spend concentrated time on spiritual issues.

- *He has made giving a part of his spiritual life.* As with most guys, giving has always been a delicate issue to him, so he has made progress by realizing that giving of his money is as much a part of his spiritual life as reading his Bible or praying. For the first time in his life, he feels that God controls his checkbook.

- *He wants to be a more effective witness.* Learning to communicate his faith has become important to him, so he's doing his best to live a life that causes people to see the hope in him. When the opportunity presents itself, he has also learned to take the time to communicate his faith verbally.

Does this guy look familiar to you? Well, if you've taken the time to apply what we've been talking about throughout this book, I have good news for you . . .

That person is you!

That's right, it's you. There's absolutely nothing in this book that you can't do. Christians who succeed at practicing the spiritual disciplines do not have an "S" sewn on their chests, nor do they have a cape that flows in the breeze as they fly over tall buildings. It's not a superman thing; it's an ordinary man thing.

Therein lies the encouragement. Typical men like you and me can see a difference in our lives as we allow the Holy Spirit to help us make the spiritual disciplines a reality.

Don't misread these words, however, for I'm not suggesting that you attempt all these disciplines immediately or that you create some sort of sanctified "to do" list. That won't work. You'll be spiritually disciplined for about a week, and then you'll be too overwhelmed to make it happen, canning the whole process.

No, I'm suggesting instead that you incorporate one spiritual discipline at a time. As each one grows and develops, take on a new one. Make this a critical year for your spiritual growth. You'll discover that you'll make fewer mistakes as time goes on.

On a recent ministry trip to South Africa, I was to preach in a black township outside Johannesburg. The men's enthusiasm as they worshiped was wonderful, even though I didn't understand their language.

Eventually they began to sing a chorus in English with which I was familiar. The words flowed as they added new verses along the way. They were singing,

"For He alone is worthy. . ."

Then they added these words:

"In Him there is no failure. . ."

What a reminder for us when we feel we've failed in the area of the disciplines! The only real failure is to walk away.

During my second year of marriage, I was attending college full-time and holding down a full-time job as well. (I say this to gain your sympathy so I don't feel like a complete fool!) In the midst of everything going on in our lives, Susan's birthday seemed to appear out of nowhere. While I remembered in the nick of time, it was apparent to all that the observance, gathering, and gift were not well thought out.

To say the least, Susan was hurt and disappointed. But she was also forgiving. It wasn't the end of our marriage but rather another step in growing together.

I could have sung,
"In her there is no failure."
She loved me, forgave me, and offered me a fresh start.

It's the same way with the Lord. We often view Him as looking down on our mess-ups, condemning us and leaving us. Yet the truth is that if we understand His grace and forgiveness, we won't beat ourselves down with false guilt, but we'll see that "in Him there is no failure." Instead we find love, forgiveness, and a fresh start.

Maybe you've tried to implement the spiritual disciplines, only to see them eroded over time. You feel like a failure, so you've covered things over with "just in time" parties and gifts. God knows and understands and offers you a fresh start—today.

A favorite poem helps me with perspective:

I had walked life's path with an easy tread,
Had followed where comfort and pleasure led;
And then by chance in a quiet place—
I met my Master face-to-face.

With station and rank and wealth for goal,
Much thought for body but none for soul,
I had entered to win this life's mad race—
When I met my Master face-to-face.

I had built my castles, reared them high,
Till their towers had pierced the blue of the sky;
I had sworn to rule with an iron mace—
When I met my Master face-to-face.

I met Him and knew Him and blushed to see,
That His eyes full of sorrow were fixed upon me;
And I faltered and fell at His feet that day,
While my castles vanished and melted away.

Melted and vanished; and in their place,
I saw naught else but my Master's face.
And I cried aloud, "Oh make me meet,
To follow the marks of Thy wounded feet."

My thought is now for the souls of men;
I have lost my life to find it again,
Ever since alone in that holy place,
My Master and I stood face-to-face.

Author Unknown

When the Lord looks at my heart, I want Him to see the heart of a godly man. How about you? Let's join together to make that a realistic goal in our lives. By keeping one another accountable, it can happen—soon.

NOTES

Chapter 1
1. John Edward Gardner, *Personal Religious Disciplines* (Grand Rapids: Eerdmans, 1966), 14.

Chapter 3
1. Richard Mayhue, *Spiritual Intimacy: Developing a Closer Relationship with God* (Wheaton, Ill.: Victor, 1990), 40.
2. R. C. Sproul, *Knowing Scripture* (Downers Grove, Ill.: InterVarsity, 1977),17.
3. Donald S. Whitney, *Spiritual Disciplines for the Christian Life* (Colorado Springs: Nav-Press, 1991), 38.
4. Ibid., 44, 55.
5. J. I. Packer in Sproul, *Knowing Scripture,* 9–10.

Chapter 4
1. John Edward Gardner, *Personal Religious Disciplines* (Grand Rapids: Eerdmans, 1966), 50.

Chapter 5
1. Richard Mayhue, *Spiritual Intimacy: Developing a Closer Relationship with God* (Wheaton, Ill.: Victor, 1990), 75.
2. Warren W. Wiersbe, *Real Worship* (Nashville: Oliver-Nelson, 1986), 27.
3. Ibid., 21.
4. A. W. Tozer, quoted in Edythe Draper, *Draper's Book of Quotations for the Christian World* (Wheaton, Ill.: Tyndale, 1992), entry 12099.
5. William Temple, Quoted in entry 12124.
6. Donald S. Whitney, *Spiritual Disciplines for the Christian Life* (Colorado Springs: Nav-Press, 1991), 81.
7. Theodore Parker, quoted in Draper, *Draper's Book of Quotations,* entry 12109.
8. Ray Ortlund, quoted in ibid entry 12137.
9. C. S. Lewis, quoted in ibid., entry 12093.
10. Erwin Lutzer, quoted in ibid., entry 12101.
11. Richard Foster, quoted in ibid., entry 12105.
12. Whitney, *Spiritual Disciplines.* 87, 89.
13. Ruth Bell Graham, quoted in Draper, *Draper's Book of Quotations,* entry 12102.

Chapter 6
1. Ron DelBene with Herb and Mary Montgomery, *Alone with God: A Guide for Personal Retreats* (Nashville: Upper Room, 1992), 11.
2. David R. Smith, *Fasting: A Neglected Discipline* (London: Hodder and Stoughton, 1954), 29.
3. William Barclay, *The Gospel According to Matthew,* vol. 1, rev. ed. (Philadelphia: Westminster, 1975), 237–38.
4. Paul Anderson, "20 Questions and Answers on Fasting," *Christian Herald,* October 1987, 30–38.

Chapter 7
1. John Edward Gardner, *Personal Religious Disciplines* (Grand Rapids: Eerdmans, 1966), 18, 22, 23.

Chapter 8
1. Donald S. Whitney, *Spiritual Disciplines for the Christian Life* (Colorado Springs: NavPress, 1991), 94.

Chapter 10
1. Gary W. Downing, "Accountability That Makes Sense," *Leadership,* Spring 1988, 42–44.

A HEART FOR GOD
EXERCISE GUIDE

BY JAMES S. BELL, JR.

Jesus told the parable of two sons who were asked to go into the vineyard. The first said he would go but didn't. The second at first refused but later went anyway. After reading this book, you may relate to either son. Perhaps you have every intention of getting serious about these spiritual disciplines, but without some concrete action points your goals will melt away. Or maybe you're like the second son in that you've been overwhelmed by the sheer magnitude of all these activities that get us closer to God. You may say, "It's a nice book, and hopefully it will have a positive effect, but I know I won't do all the author suggests."

These exercises provide the framework to follow through for both types of men. In the first case, you can put feet to your confidence and follow through. In the second case, you can choose which questions or activities you can handle and then have a specific way to manage it at your own level and pace. Even as I get excited about carrying out many of these suggestions, my friend Glenn reminds me in the tenth chapter not to attempt all these disciplines at once. I'll be doing great for about a week and then be overwhelmed and give up. So take all my seeming commands in this series of questions as helpful suggestions—between you and the Lord. And I hope you'll discuss them with other men as well, because they are best achieved in a group setting.

INTRODUCTION

1. How would you describe your own stereotype of a super-saint? What characteristics of spirituality may not be accurate—that is, superficial, misleading, or unbiblical?

2. Describe the intimacy you have with your spouse or closest friend. How did you get to know that person deeply and thoroughly? How could this be applied to knowing Christ?

3. If you had to measure the depth of your friendship with Christ according to the author's descriptions, where would you presently place it along the spectrum—initial, social, close, or intimate—and why?

4. Look at the following six essentials for intimacy in a relationship.

- confidence
- confrontation

- counsel
- companionship
- consistency
- commitment

Rather than rating yourself, how would you say the Lord has fulfilled these qualities toward you? What does that prove about His friendship?

5. Now consider Dr. Rod Cooper's six qualities needed to move from isolation to intimacy. Which one is your greatest strength? Which one gives you the greatest difficulty? Why is delayed gratification in this list?

6. Look at the difference between the author's experience with the trumpet and his daughter's efforts in figure skating. What skills have you undertaken that require discipline? In this example, were you closer to father or daughter? Why?

CHAPTER ONE

1. Review the list of "ordinary" guys that God used in extra-ordinary ways for His purposes. Go to the Scriptures and find another character similar to those in this list. Where were his weaknesses, and how did God use him?

2. Whether it's politics, sports, or any number of other concerns, what brings out your strong opinions and deep commitment? What allowed you to become knowledgeable and/or successful in these areas?

3. How does the issue of spiritual growth compare with the other "passionate" areas of your life? What de-motivates or turns you off (makes you apathetic) about the topic? What causes your ups and downs? What's the "hook" that gets you most excited?

4. Do a quick review of the book of Galatians, and see how they turned spiritual growth into a set of rules instead of a spiritual relationship based on grace. When and how have you or

others taken the same legalistic approach to acceptance in the past? Why did it fail?

5. How is it that we can be freed from the power of sin if we still sin from time to time? What happened to us with the death of Christ? What is the power now at work in us? Write a paragraph on how these answers help us with the spiritual disciplines.

6. How can you be freed from the power of God's law if His law is good? Why will your own efforts only produce bondage and guilt? (Hint: The answers are also found in the book of Romans.) Why are your efforts still a vital part of success in the spiritual disciplines?

CHAPTER TWO

1. Obedience often seems hard and even foolish at times. Our way seems so much better and yet falls short. Think of a time when the consequences of disobedience were accompanied by a heavy price. Why?

2. Now look at the blessings (perhaps even unexpected) of simple obedience to God's commands in your own life. Even at times when things didn't make sense, what were some of the beneficial results?

3. We cannot create our own integrity; rather, it's a by-product of yielding to God's will and power regularly. When has your moral character been severely tested and God has in turn sustained you? How has your commitment to Him made a difference?

4. What would you describe as the major area in your thought life that is not consistent with God's Word? Rather than

just fighting it, what corresponding true, honorable, and pure thoughts (Philippians 4:7–8) might replace these improper thoughts?

5. Think back to a time when one of your children (if you have any) performed a deed of strong character. What influence did you have? What could you do (or have done) that would be a positive influence for the character development of other family members?

6. If you were on your deathbed today, what would be your regrets? What words or deeds would you have increased or decreased? Make a decision to immediately speak to or do something for someone that is more in line with the person you really want to be.

7. If you left this world tomorrow, what would your family and those closest to you say they missed most about you? What would they miss least? Finally, what do you think they would say about your potential for greater things as a giving, loving person?

CHAPTER THREE

1. Write an imaginative account of your own Bible's diary. What would it say regarding your intentions and actions over the last week? How was it handled, and where did it reside? Now write your Bible's story of you as you really want it to be.

2. Many of us find at least some of God's commands difficult or even burdensome. Yet David delighted in His commands and investigated them constantly. How do we experience His love within His commands rather than experiencing the fear of failure or punishment?

3. Without assurance, your Christian walk will be, among other things, uncertain, out of balance, and lukewarm. List as many as ten areas (examples: salvation, God's presence) where you want assurance. Now go to your Bible (get help if you need it) and find the promises that guarantee them.

4. We are in bondage in many ways—addictions, fears, failures, and so on. Yet we're promised complete freedom from those powers. Find a few verses that demonstrate freedom from wrong attitudes, behavior, and both the hold and consequences of the power of sin.

5. Have you ever felt squeamish about discussing or defending your faith? Could part of it be the fear of being overwhelmed in a discussion by a skeptic, or even appearing ignorant when it comes to simple questions? Ask others for material that will help you understand better the truths of the Bible.

6. Scrutinize carefully the following list of spiritual experiences related to interacting with God's Word. Underline at least one important point, and make an attempt in your calendar over the next month to take at least some small steps with three disciplines:

- Bible reading
- Bible memorization
- Bible study
- Bible meditation
- Listening to a sermon

CHAPTER FOUR

1. There are many benefits of prayer, and perhaps one of the greatest is purpose in life. How has God made clear to you His calling and major life direction at crucial times through prayer? When have your mistakes in direction related to a lack of prayer?

2. Answered prayer can depend somewhat on your motive. How have some of your desires been related to self-interest as opposed to God's glory? Why are His answers sometimes painful? What is God trying to do in some of the cases where we receive an answer we may not like?

3. What holds you back from believing God for big things? Is it past disappointments, a lack of biblical knowledge of God's power, or some other reason? Pray for a greater measure of faith combined with a greater knowledge of His Word and will.

4. A big barrier to answered prayer is unconfessed sin, either individual transgressions or ongoing habits. Are there private

areas that you have not surrendered to God in your thought life (and beyond) that perhaps you've never linked to unanswered prayer or seeming distance from Him? If so, will you give them to Him now? Why or why not?

5. Take the four main areas of prayer—strength, salvation, physical and material needs, and workers for the harvest—and incorporate them in your personal prayer life over the next month. Be specific as the Lord leads you in these areas. Now pick a fifth area of your own based on a Scripture verse related to prayer in some way.

6. ACTS is the acronym for the four most important subdivisions of prayer, none of which should be left out of your prayer life. On a piece of paper, write the acronym vertically down the left side, and then make thirty copies. Each day for the next month, on one of those copies, try to list at least one thing each under adoration, confession, thanksgiving, and supplication. Watch how your prayers improve over time.

CHAPTER FIVE

1. Name the place, source, or set of circumstances that cause you to worship most profoundly. What is it that allows you to see some aspect of God clearly and that you truly appreciate? What is your favorite part of worship, that which draws you closest to Him?

2. Sundays are not the only time to worship God. What excuses do you make for lack of private devotions, participation in midweek services, small groups, and so on? What does this show you about your true priorities in regard to worship? How can you overcome these excuses?

3. In what ways do we bring God down to our level, reducing His holiness and thus diminishing true worship? Read the accounts in Revelation where those who are in the presence of God worship Him. What words and phrases do they use as a result of that holy vision?

4. Write out your own expression of worship, giving to God what is due His name, recounting His deeds and the way you feel about Him. Ask Him to reveal at a deep level in your spirit all of His awesome qualities so that you may better worship.

5. What have been your own most memorable life-changing experiences of worship? How did they change you from the inside? Why is it that some worship services or exercises, though using biblical "formulas," don't seem to cause change or growth? What aspect of God do you enjoy and reverence most?

6. Are there any church, family, or private "spiritual" activities that don't incorporate much true worship but really should? How could you take steps to accelerate worship in the right settings? What contribution could you make?

CHAPTER SIX

1. What scares you about silence? In what ways might you fear being alone with God? Might it be facing judgment, lack of direction, commands you don't want, boredom, rejection, or something else? Give this to the Lord in prayer, and ask for a deeper desire than ever to spend regular time with Him.

2. Even if you have a phobia, every Christian has benefited from times alone with God. List the great things that have come from even brief periods of solitude—assurances of God's love, major decisions made, prayers answered, and so on. Why were both time and being alone necessary?

3. Set a place and time, with protections built in, where you will spend a full day (preferably overnight) seeking the Lord, especially listening. Write out an agenda ahead of time that will include prayer, Scripture reading, worship, seeking His guidance, and so on. Consider the options of fasting and journaling as well.

4. Rather than making a long-term commitment to journaling, begin by writing to the Lord whatever is on your heart just three times per week over the next month. Rather than a certain number of words, allow a short time where you won't feel overwhelmed.

5. Now, at least in this first phase, experiment with a different focus for each of these weeks—spiritual readings, emotional life, encounters with God, and others. At the end of that period, determine which is the most satisfying and why.

6. Between William Barclay and Paul Anderson, the chapter presents twelve points in favor of fasting. Write these twelve positives on a piece of paper, and add a note of explanation about why you agree. Based on that admittance, commit to a full or partial list in order to grow closer to God within the next month.

CHAPTER SEVEN

1. Do you accept the fact that everything you own belongs to God, even your body? Surrender anything that you are retaining to be used according to your own discretion. Commit everything to God, and pray that He will direct you in terms of managing His resources. What haven't you surrendered?

2. Recall the instances where God has supplied your needs over and above normal means. When have you truly been deprived of any need? Do you pray first regarding what you need? Make a list of your needs, but first commit to use them God's way; then pray.

3. In terms of what you do give, rate yourself regarding your motivation, as well as actual exercise or experience, in these areas:

- thanksgiving
- submission to God
- experience joy
- receive a heavenly reward
- support the work of the gospel
- help meet others' needs

• faith in God's supply

4. In light of this chapter, seek to arrive at a systematic plan for giving that will establish a minimum amount to build upon regardless of personal circumstances. Establish what stretches beyond your circumstances; that is, define what "generous" and "sacrificial" mean in your case, and stay with it by faith.

5. Tithing is difficult for many people. The author gives a number of reasons why it's beneficial: for instance, God is glorified. Find the one argument that is most compelling, and write up to a page about why this makes sense. Keep this in mind when you doubt or are tempted to cut back on your giving.

6. Talk to at least three people who tithe. Ask them what has happened to their lives as a result of this discipline. How has God met their needs and beyond? How might they compare their life now to the time when they didn't tithe? What does this say to you?

CHAPTER EIGHT

1. What earthly things are you passionate about that you discuss with others? Why do you want others to reap benefits and joy similar to what you have experienced? What takes away your shyness even if the other person might not be interested?

2. Where are your lifestyle and character in relation to your witness? Even though you focus on Christ, others want to know how He has made a difference for you. What changes do you need to make now that will help the effectiveness of your witness? Don't, however, use an imperfect life as an excuse not to witness.

3. Choose two individuals who seem to be open to the faith and with whom you can develop a close relationship. Based upon your service and love to them, develop a plan to speak to them about the source of your life within the next six months. Pray for a genuine interest in them as people, not merely as lost souls.

4. How can you better become a part of your unsaved friends' worlds without compromising your faith or falling into sin? By reaching out, how do you maintain purity and a separated life? Analyze the temptations you may fall into ahead of time if you immerse yourself in a deep friendship.

5. Critique your past witnessing efforts, or if you have never witnessed, write on a piece of paper how you would handle the following five points:

- consistency
- nonthreatening friendship
- leading of the Holy Spirit
- simple and clear message
- a godly life

Where do you tend to fail or be unbalanced? What area would you describe as your strongest point, and why? Apply these specifically to key relationships with unbelievers.

6. Look at the poem at the end of the chapter. How does this affect your earnestness to bring souls to Christ? Though we can't save anyone, if we don't present the gospel, others may perish for eternity. Hang a copy of this poem on your wall as you pray for courage to discuss the gospel with those lost souls around you.

CHAPTER NINE

1. Go back to each spiritual discipline discussed in this book: Bible study, prayer, worship, solitude and fasting, giving, and witnessing. Look at the following considerations for being able to do a thorough job in each discipline.

2. Set aside real time in your organizer or calendar to do the exercises mentioned in this study guide. Ultimately, you cannot afford to eliminate any of them, so be realistic but sacrificing as you carve out long-term schedules to make progress in each discipline. Build in a cushion for interruptions so you can come back at a later period to resume.

3. What will it take to cultivate the mental, emotional, and physical stamina as well as determination necessary to follow through to the completion of each of these tasks on a regular basis? Measure your own energy level in terms of adding on these increased activities. How can you change other commitments to accommodate these vital exercises?

4. Make an attempt to obtain the printed material necessary to do further background study on each of these disciplines. Try to secure a quiet location with adequate space, lighting, reference books for Bible study, journals, and perhaps even a computer to save your notes. Make it a place that supports inspiration, creativity, and concentration.

5. Assemble an informal accountability group of men who are like-minded in regard to the spiritual disciplines. Stay in contact once a month, and clearly articulate your goals. Allow them to both encourage and correct you if necessary. If you do this alone, it's easy to fail. Give yourself some cushion for failure so it will not be an excuse to quit.

6. Before beginning this new series of spiritual disciplines, seek God for a deep hunger and passion both to know Him better and to become a godly man. Without either the initial fire within or the ability to visualize the end results, your enthusiasm will wane. Write a description of the kind of intimate relationship you will have with Christ, as well as the kind of person you will become.

7. Go back and review the activities you have agreed to begin or expand upon in the previous exercises. If, as a whole, they now appear overwhelming, develop an "accelerated stages" approach. Though you're not discarding the commitment to the long haul, success in the first, smaller stage will encourage you to move ahead.

CHAPTER TEN

1. Like the football player in the huddle, describe an environment where you felt energized and encouraged to make a contribution as part of a team. It might be in church, a hobby, a sport, or a social event. What were the group dynamics that allowed you to do your best? What did you accomplish?

2. How might the success of this group dynamic mentioned above apply to a men's group that fosters the spiritual disciplines? What elements of mutual encouragement or motivation could transfer to a group like this? Could some of the same individuals be "transplanted" to this men's group?

3. A leader, or at least a competent moderator, is important for a successful men's group. If it's not you, can you think of someone capable of advising (or actually leading) a new men's small group? Begin to inquire and perhaps, in a nonthreatening way, start approaching him with the idea.

4. All of us have some fears about accountability. Failure, self-esteem, and other issues enter the picture, as well as perhaps some past hurts. List these in a candid, transparent way before the Lord, and if necessary, before your future (or present) small group members. Ask God to deal with these areas in the right way.

5. Apart from the accountability issue, what other areas of small groups as a whole may bother you? Create two columns divided into pros and cons. List past failures or fears, and then list all the encouragement, improved relationships, and creative input from the group. Can you afford to go it alone with the spiritual disciplines?

6. Do your castles stand tall or crumble as you stand face-to-face with your Master? Have you even tried good works without much of a face-to-face relationship with Him? The Lord will not condemn you, and there is still time. Tell God through a written commitment that as a result of this book, you will work to become a godly man in every area of your life—to make your first priority knowing Him, by His grace!